I0830170

PREFACE

It is obvious that poor hazardous area classification or undermining the risk of flammable, explosive or toxic atmosphere has caused havoc in our societies and world at large. Human lives, oil & gas installations, chemical companies etc. have in the recent times burnt down due to negligence to acknowledge or not being aware of deadly hazards in form of gas, vapour, or dust within and around the area of operation. Also, many lives have lost due to inhalation of toxic gas like H2S, CO and their like because many are inadvertently not aware of the dangers of the deadly toxic gases in environment.

This book *"Awareness on Toxic, Flammable and Explosive Atmosphere"* is authored to bridge the gap. It is a born out desire to solve one of the world's greatest challenges – sudden death and loss of Assets due to the presence of flammable, explosive or toxic atmosphere.

Within the context of this book Hazardous Area Classification is defined as an assessed division of a plant or facility into hazardous and non-hazardous areas and the sub-division of hazardous area into zones. Hazardous zones include: 0, 1, and 2 for gas environment and 20, 21 and 22 for dust environment and their corresponding equipment category 1, 2, & 3 gas and M1 & M2 for dust respectively. These zones in relationship to types of explosive atmosphere they form give rise to types of protection the facility and environs requires taken cognizance the type of gas or dust detection equipment.

Degree of Emission and ventilation affect the behaviour of hazardous atmosphere and plays a great role either to increase concentration or reduce concentration of flammable or explosive atmosphere.

"*Awareness on Toxic, Flammable and Explosive Atmosphere*" x-rayed zones of hazardous area classifications and equipment category making it easy to comprehend. It offers a great deal to understand hazardous atmosphere better and need to make a good assessment that would be suitable for a particular facility base on prevalent flammable, explosive and toxic gasses.

Also, it considered the importance of Auto-ignition Temperature and flash points of materials and equipment as essentials keeping in mind the auto-ignition temperature of the expected hazards from the facility.

This book state emphatically the essentiality of Temperature class of equipment & materials to avert installing equipment and materials that would end up generating spark or heat that could destroy the entire facility.

Furthermore, it provides detail explanation on Ingress Protection and it significance in Hazardous Area Classification.

Finally, let us keep our environment free from toxic, flammable and explosive atmosphere.

TABLE OF CONTENTS

CHAPTER ONE

HAZARDOUS AREA CLASSIFICATION (HAC)

Hazardous Area Classification is the assessed division of a plant or facility into hazardous and non-hazardous areas and the sub-division of hazardous area into zones.

The essence of Hazards Area Classification (HAC) is to provide a basis for the selection and provision of equipment appropriate to the defined areas and to avoid ignition of flammable fluid or explosive atmosphere.

1.1 TYPE OF HAZARD

The hazard may be in form of:

1. gas,
2. Vapour and
3. Dust or fiber.

GAS: A substance whose boiling point at atmospheric pressure is below normal ambient temperature. Gases take the shape and volume of their enclosure.

VAPOUR: Vapour is formed by evaporation of the substance and can be condensed back to the normal state by change in either pressure or temperature; a temperature rise will cause vaporization i.e. petrol, solvents, mercury.

Dust: Airborne particulate matter ranging in diameter from 10 to 50 microns, generated by activities such as cutting, crushing, detonation, grinding, and handling of organic and inorganic matter such as coal, grain, metal, ore, rock, wood. Their presence in atmosphere can create an explosive atmosphere.

CHAPTER TWO

DEGREE OF EMISSION

The degree of emission represents the probability that an emission source emits gas, liquid, or vapour such as to create a potentially explosive atmosphere.

- **Continuous emission:** continuous emission or emission for long periods.
- **Primary emission:** periodic or occasional emission during normal operation.
- **Secondary emission:** emission which is unlikely during normal operation or which occurs only rarely or for short periods.

The type of zone is strictly related to the degree of emission; in general, a continuous emission generates a zone '0', a primary emission generates a zone '1' and secondary emission generates a zone '2'.

The ventilation is the element that can change this correspondence, as poor ventilation or lack of ventilation could aggravate the classification of the zone (e.g. a primary emission could then lead to a zone 0 instead of a zone 1).

CHAPTER THREE

VENTILATION & BEHAVIOUR OF HAZARDOUS ATMOSPHERE

It is the movement of air or its replacement with fresh air produced by the wind, a thermal gradient or artificial means (the use of fans or extractor units).

The gases or vapours which can create an explosive atmosphere can be diluted in the air, thereby dropping below the minimum hazard levels; thus efficient ventilation allows to obtain a reduction of the hazardous zone. The ventilation can be distinguished based on its efficiency and availability.

The following degrees of ventilation have been identified:

- **High ventilation (HV):** when the ventilation is able to reduce the concentration of hazardous gas below the lower explosive limit (LEL) almost immediately.

- **Medium ventilation (MV):** when the ventilation is able to affect the concentration of gas in a stable manner, lowering the concentration below the LEL or where the hazardous atmosphere persists for a short period.

- **Low ventilation (LV):** when the ventilation is unable to affect the concentration of gas in a stable manner and is incapable of persistently limiting a hazardous atmosphere.

In addition to the degree of ventilation, the efficiency of a ventilation system also depends on its availability; the presence of high ventilation (HV) may be thwarted by its scarce availability (e.g. a faulty fan).

AVAILABILITY OF VENTILATION

- **Good ventilation:** when the ventilation is present continuously.

- **Adequate ventilation:** when the ventilation is present during normal operation; infrequent interruptions for short periods are allowed.

- **Poor ventilation:** when the ventilation is not able to meet the requirements in order to be considered good or adequate; in any case no long-lasting interruptions are expected.

CHAPTER FOUR

HAZARDOUS AREA CLASSIFICATION CRITERIA

The classification of the areas with risk of explosion is a rather complex procedure, but it is essentially based on the identification of the following elements:

- **Number and position of the emission sources (ES)**

- **Type of emission sources:** degree, emission flow rate.

- **Degree of ventilation:** high (HV), medium (MV), low (LV).

- **Availability of ventilation:** good, adequate or poor.

- The **(auto) ignition temperature** of the hazardous material

The elements cited above led, by means of calculations and other assessments, to the definition of the hazardous zones and relative extensions. Generally the hazardous zones are represented on the installation designs using the graphic symbols shown below.

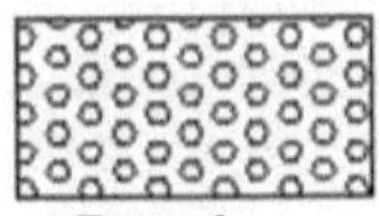
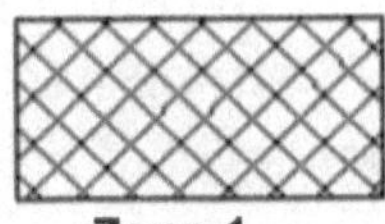

| Zone 0 | Zone 1 | Zone 2 |

Although there is no fixed rule regarding the presence (duration and probability) of explosive atmosphere in relation to the zones (0, 1, 2), the following table represents a useful reference.

CHAPTER FIVE

CLASSIFICATION OF EQUIPMENT

5.1 GROUPS AND CATEGORIES:

Group I: Intended for use in the underground parts of mines likely to become endangered by firedamp and/or combustible duct

Group II: Intended for use in other places (surface facilities like oil and gas installation, chemical industries etc.), likely to become endangered by explosive/flammable atmosphere.

5.2 EQUIPMENT CATEGORY UNDER GROUP I

Directive 94/9/EC classifies the products in categories, in relation to the level of protection and based on the degree of risks to the environment where they will be installed.

Equipment under Group I is subdivided into Category M1, & M2.

Category M1: Equipment designed and, where necessary, equipped with additional special means of protection to be capable of functioning in conformity with the operational parameters established by the manufacturer and ensuring a very high level of protection.

Category M2: Equipment designed to be capable of functioning in conformity with the operational parameters established by the manufacturer and ensuring a high level of protection.

LEVEL OF PROTECTION	CATEGORY		PERFORMANCE OF PROTECTION	CONDITIONS OF OPERATION*
	GROUP I	GROUP II		
Very High	M 1		Two independent means of protection or safe even when two faults occur independently of each other.	Equipment remains energised and functioning when explosive atmosphere present
Very High		1	Two independent means of protection or safe even when two faults occur independently of each other.	Equipment remains energised and functioning in Zones 0,1,2 (G) and/or 20, 21, 22 (D)
High	M 2		Suitable for normal operation and severe operating conditions. If applicable also suitable for frequently occurring disturbances or for faults which are normally taken into account.	Equipment de-energised when explosive atmosphere is recognised
High		2	Suitable for normal operation and frequently occurring disturbances or equipment where faults are normally taken into account.	Equipment remains energised and functioning in Zones 1, 2 (G) and/or 21, 22 (D)
Normal		3	Suitable for normal operation.	Equipment remains energised and functioning in Zone 2 (G) and/or 22 (D)

Note: see as well the directives on minimum requirements for improving the safety and health protection of workers operating in potentially explosive atmospheres, e.g. those indicated in footnote 7. The equipment in the various categories must also comply with the relevant essential and supplementary requirements detailed in Annex II to the Directive (Essential Health and Safety Requirements).

5.3 EQUIPMENT CATEGORY UNDER GROUP II

Equipment under group II is subdivided into Category I, II & III.

Category 1: For use in areas in which explosive atmospheres are present continuously for long period or frequently.

Category 2: For use in areas in which explosive atmospheres are likely to occur.

Category 3: for use in areas in which explosive atmospheres are unlikely or occur only infrequently and for a short period

CHAPTER SIX

HAZARDOUS AREA CLASSIFICATION ZONES FOR GAS

The likelihood of the hazard being present in flammable and in explosive concentrations will vary from place to place. A location very close to an open source of hazard will have a high likelihood of a flammable or explosive atmosphere. Rather than work with an infinite range of possibilities, three zones are defined. In the same vein, fuel storage areas, dispensing area and environs have varying flammable or explosive concentrations.

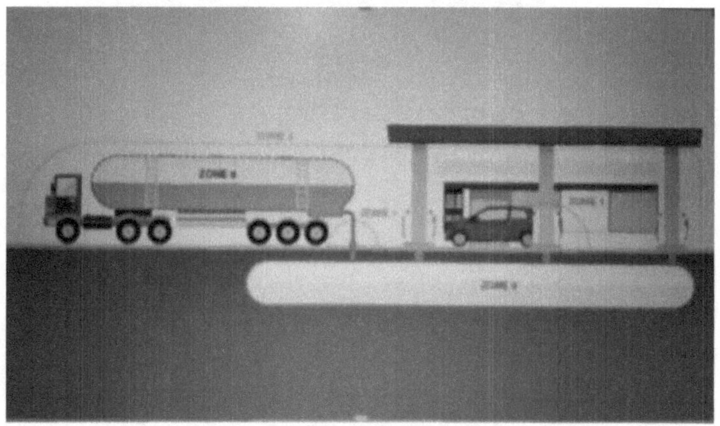

6.1 EQUIPMENT CATEGORY AND ZONES
The hazardous area zone classification and corresponding equipment category
Categories are:
Category 1 equipment is suitable for Zone 0, 1 & 2
Category 2 equipment is suitable for Zone 1 & 2
Category 3 equipment is suitable only for zone 2

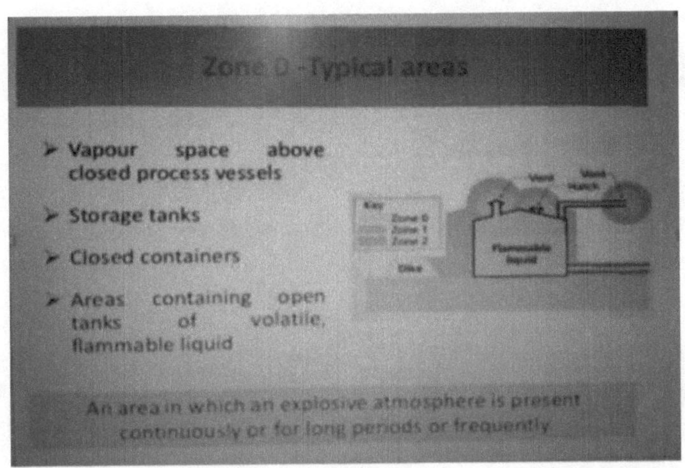

Zone 0	Flammable atmosphere highly likely to be present - may be present for long periods or even continuously
Zone 1	Flammable atmosphere possible but unlikely to be present for long periods. A location in which explosive gas atmospheres are likely to exist in normal operation or may exist frequently because of repairs, maintenance operations, and leakage or where equipment breakdowns could release gases or vapours.
Zone 2	Flammable atmosphere unlikely to be present except for short periods of time - typically as a result of a process fault condition.

Zone zero is the most severe zone (the highest probability of flammable atmosphere presence). Equipment for this zone needs to be very well protected against providing a source of ignition.

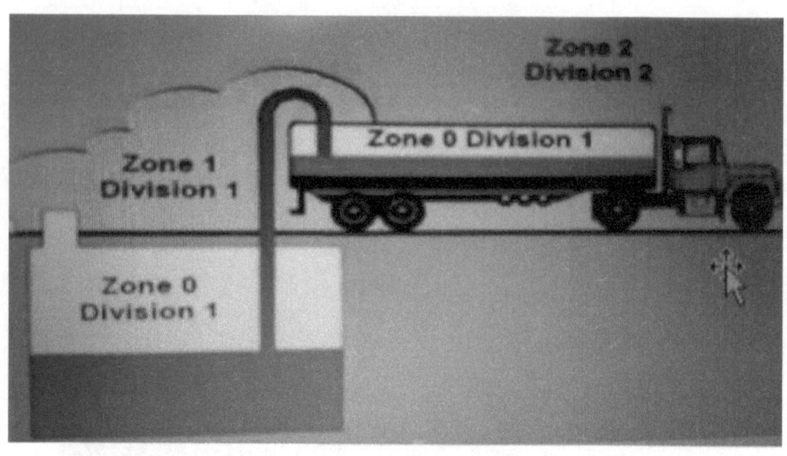

6.2 SUITABLE ELECTRICAL EQUIPMENT

The electrical equipment installed in the zones classified for gas must conform to the ATEX Directive 94/9/EC and must be suitable for the hazardous zones as shown in the table below:

Hazardous zone		Directive 94/9/EC category
Gas and vapours	Zone 0	1G
Gas and vapours	Zone 1	2G or 1G
Gas and vapours	Zone 2	3G or 2G or 1G

CHAPTER SEVEN

HAZARDOUS AREA CLASSIFICATION ZONES FOR DUST

The classification of the areas with risk of explosion due to the presence of dust is made in a manner similar to that provided for gas, based on the probability of the presence of an explosive atmosphere.

7.1 DUST ZONE CLASSIFICATION

The standard IEC EN 61241-10 defines three zones:

Zone 20: A place in which an explosive atmosphere under the form of combustible dust in the air is present continuously, frequently or for long periods.

Zone 21: A place in which an explosive atmosphere under the form of combustible dust in the air is likely to occur under normal operation occasionally.

Zone 22: A place in which an explosive atmosphere under the form of combustible dust in the air is not likely to occur under normal operation but, if it does occur, it will persist for only a short period of time.

Graphic symbols of the classified zones for dusts:

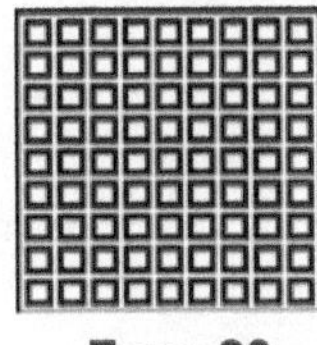 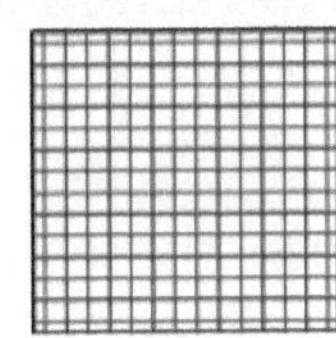 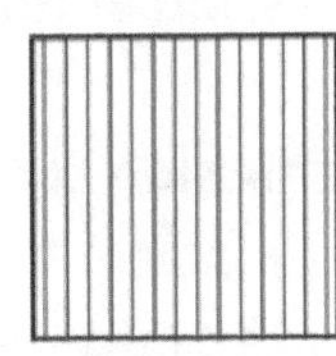

| Zone 20 | Zone 21 | Zone 22 |

7.2 SOME EXAMPLES OF POSSIBLE HAZARDOUS ZONE SITUATIONS FOR DUSTS

Zone	Examples
Zone 20	Filters, cyclones. Dust transport systems, interiors of mixers, mills, dryers, desiccators.
Zone 21	Zones outside hoppers. Areas near filling and emptying points.
Zone 22	Dust transport systems, interiors of mixers, mills, dryers, desiccators. Areas near equipment that is opened occasionally.

7.3 SOME DEFINITIONS

Combustible dusts
Dust capable of burning in air and forming explosive mixtures with air at atmospheric pressure and normal temperatures.

Dust containment
Parts of the process equipment within which the dust is handled, treated, transported or stored, e.g., to prevent the emission of dust into the surrounding atmosphere.

Date emission source
Point or place from which the combustible dust may be emitted into the atmosphere.

7.4 DUST ZONE CLASSIFICATION CRITERIA

The classification for dusts is also a complex procedure that requires the identification of the type, the number and degree of the emission sources. Occasionally, depending on the installation conditions, the introduction of ventilation may allow some areas to be classified as zone 22 which would otherwise be considered as zone 21.

7.5 SUITABLE ELECTRICAL EQUIPMENT

The electrical equipment installed in the classified zones must conform to the ATEX Directive 94/9/EC and must be suitable for the hazardous zones as shown in the table below:

Hazardous zone		Directive 94/9/EC category
Dusts	Zone 20	1D
Dusts	Zone 21	2D or 1D
Dusts	Zone 22	3D or 2D or 1D

CHAPTER EIGHT

EQUIPMENT SELECTION

The equipment must be selected based on the hazardous zone, the substances present, the ignition temperatures and the environmental characteristics of the installation locations.

Hazardous zone

The selection must be made considering the equipment category (ATEX 94/9/EC) which must be SUITABLE for the type of zone (ATEX 99/92/EC).

Hazardous zone		Directive 94/9/EC category
Gas and vapours	Zone 0	1G
Gas and vapours	Zone 1	2G or 1G
Gas and vapours	Zone 2	3G or 2G or 1G
Dusts	Zone 20	1D
Dusts	Zone 21	2D or 1D
Dusts	Zone 22	3D or 2D or 1D

Note G stands for Gas & D stands for Dust under their various equipment categories

CHAPTER NINE
SUBSTANCES

The various substances have different explosive behaviours. The group II electrical equipment, for gas and vapours, is divided into subgroups IIA, IIB and IIC in relation to the substance. Group IIC is the **most restrictive** and the group IIA is the **least restrictive**. Based on the substance, it is possible to identify the group to which the equipment must belong.

The electrical equipment certified for a certain gas group can also be used, for safety, in the locations where equipment of a less restrictive group is suitable. In other terms:

- An apparatus of the group IIB can be used in places which require an apparatus of the group IIA;
- An apparatus of the group IIC can be used in places which require an apparatus of the groups IIA and IIB.

Occasionally, an apparatus is indicated as suitable for a gas group (IIB for example) and for a certain gas of the subsequent group, hydrogen for example; in this case the apparatus is marked as **IIB + H_2**.

Gases and vapours are categorized in terms of their ignition energy or the maximum experimental safe gap (in respect of flameproof protection). This categorization leads to the Gas Groups:

Mining	Surface Industry		
Group I	Group II		
Methane	IIA	IIB	IIC
	Propane	Ethylene	Hydrogen

(The gases noted in the table are typical gases for each group.)

Group IIC is the most severe group. Hazards in this group can be ignited very easily indeed.

CHAPTER TEN

EXPLOSIVE ATMOSPHERE

A mixture of air and one or more substances in the form of gases, vapors, mists or dust under atmospheric conditions in which combustion rapidly spreads to the entire unburned mixture after ignition.

Atmospheric conditions are commonly referred to as ambient temperatures and pressures, that is to say, temperatures of −20°C to 40°C and pressures of 0.8 to 1.1 bar. Many workplaces may contain, or have activities that produce explosive or potentially explosive atmospheres. Examples include places where work activities create or release flammable gases or vapours, such as vehicle, paint spraying, or in workplaces handling fine organic dusts such as grain flour or wood and oil & gas facilities.

Explosive atmospheres occur when flammable gases, mist, vapours or dust are mixed with air. This creates a risk of explosion. The amount of a substance needed to create an explosive atmosphere depends on the substance in question. The area where this possibility exists is defined as a potentially explosive atmosphere. These atmospheres can be found throughout all industries, from chemical, pharmaceutical and food, to power generation and wood processing. The areas may also be known as hazardous areas or hazardous locations. The number of substances that are flammable when mixed with air is very large. This means there are many industrial sectors that can have a potentially explosive atmosphere somewhere in their process. Some of these are not so obvious. For example, sawmills by default are not a potentially explosive atmosphere, but if the sawdust is allowed to gather in large amounts, the area in question will become hazardous.

10.1 EXPLOSIVE LIMITS: The range within a mixture of gas or vapor and air undergoes combustion or explodes. The explosive limits of gases and the vapors of liquid and solids are denoted by the % volume in air

10.2 LOWER EXPLOSIVE LIMIT: The lowest concentration, or percentage, of a gas or a vapor is capable of igniting and exploding in presence of an ignition source. Concentrations lower than the lower explosive limit (LEL) are 'too lean' to burn.

10.3 UPPER EXPLOSIVE LIMIT: The highest concentration or percentage of a gas or a vapor in air that is capable of igniting source. Concentration higher than the Upper Explosive Limit (UEL) are "too rich" to burn. The UEL is also known as the upper flammable limit (UFL)

10.4 PARTS PER MILLION (ppm): parts per million expresses the number of parts of a particular component in one million parts of air. On a volume/volume. It is extensively used where the concentrations are below
10 ppm = 0.001% by volume
10000 ppm = 1.0% by volume

CHAPTER ELEVEN

LIMITS OF FLAMABILITY

The extremes of gas or vapor to air ratios between which the mixture is combustible. The explosive or flammable range lies between the LEL and UEL. Below the LEL the mixture has too much air to allow combustion to take place, i.e. a lean or weak mixture. Above the UEL the mixture has too much fuel for combustion to take place, i.e. it is a too rich to support combustion.

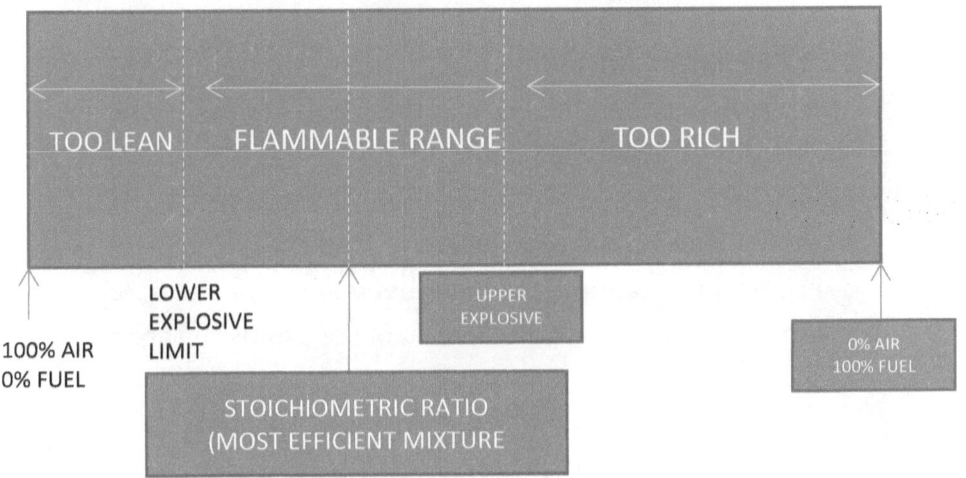

EXPLOSIVE LIMITS

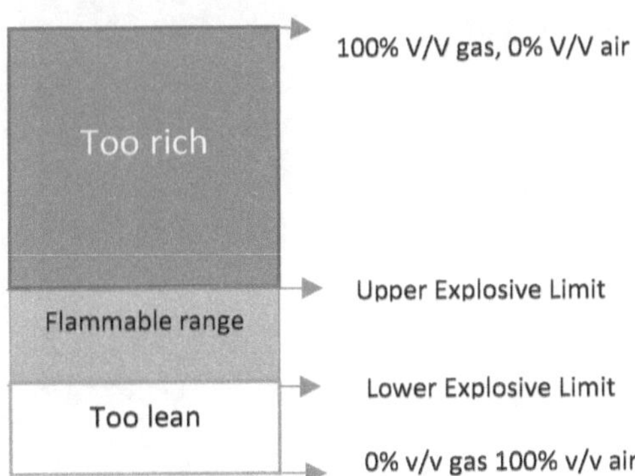

Each gas/ air mixture is ignitable over its flammable range.

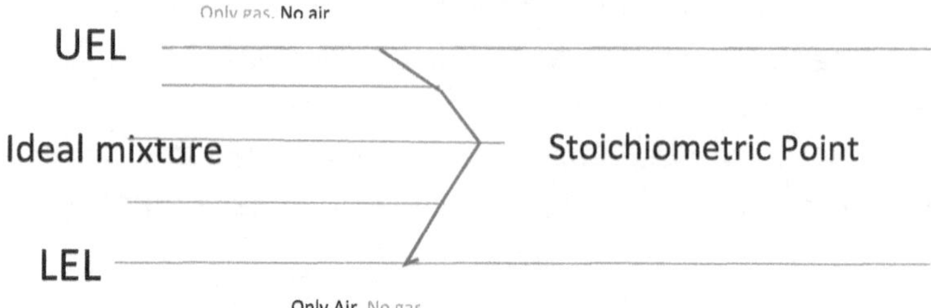

11.1 EXPLOSIVE RANGE

The region between the LEL and the UEL is known as the flammable or explosive range.

For example, the LEL of methane is 5% by volume and UEL of methane in air is 15% by volume. Thus the concentrations of methane in air between 5 and 15% are combustible and this is the flammable of Explosive range of methane.

11.2 STOICHIOMETRIC POINT

The Stoichiometric point is the ideal fuel/air mixture which gives complete combustion

Note: Stoichiometric concentration is roughly 2 X LEL

CHAPTER TWELVE

DETECTION OF FLAMMABLE/EXPLOSIVE ATMOSPHERE

Flammable gas detection meters, both fixed and portable are calibrated to read a percentage of the Lower Explosive Limit (LEL). Therefore a reading of 100% LEL means the gas will burn. We calibrate the meter using a mixture of methane. In air 5.0% volume of methane in air is equal to 100% LEL

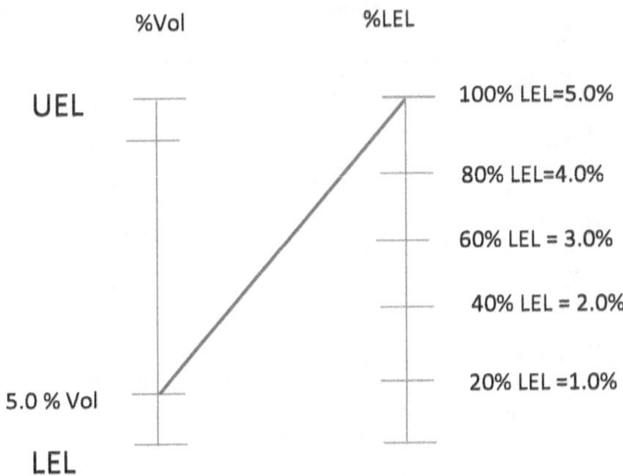

In general terms, Low level flammable gas detection alarms are set at approximately 10% LEL with high gas alarm set around 50% LEL.

Even with a high level gas alarm (at 50% LEL) the mixture is too lean to burn- at the point of detection - however, it may well be within the flammable envelope at other areas adjacent to the source. It is therefore vital that all releases of gases are rectified promptly and efficiently.

Calibration of flammable gas detectors is normally proved at the setting of 50% LEL with a test gas typically 2.5% CH4 in air. The reason for this is that 100% LEL = 5.0% CH4 in air, therefore a setting of 50% LEL = (5.0 /100) x 50 = 2.5% CH4 in air.

12.1 PERCENTAGE OF LEL and UEL OF SOME SUBSTANCE

Substance	Formula	LEL (Vol %)	UEL (Vol %)
Acetone	CH_3CHO	2.15	13.0
Acetylene	C_2H_2	2.4	88.0
Butane	C_4H_4	1.5	8.5
Ethane	C_2H_6	3.0	15.5
Ethylene	C_2H_4	2.7	34.0
Hexane	C_6H_{12}	1.2	7.4
Hydrogen	H_2	4.0	75.6
Methane	CH_4	5.0	15.0
Propane	C_3H_8	2.0	9.5

Gas detector is a device which can sample the air and detect a variety of contaminant gases, flammable and check for oxygen concentration in a given environment. It measures the concentration of a gas or gases and gives an alarm when the gas concentration reaches a present threshold value. It enables the detection of gases prior to the commencement of an operation, during and after an operation. The measurement looks at the lower explosive limit (LEL); above the pre-set LEL value, the detector bleeps indicating the presence of the set combustible gas.

Many people have probably seen a flame safety lamp at some time and know something about its use as an early form of 'firedamp' gas detector in underground coal mines and sewers. Although originally intended as a source of light, the device could also be used to estimate the level of combustible gases- to an accuracy of about 25-50%, depending on the user's experience, training, age, colour perception etc.

Modern combustible gas detectors have to be much more accurate, reliable and repeatable than this and although various attempts were made to overcome the safety lamp's subjective measurement (by using a flame temperature sensor for instance), it has now been almost entirely superseded by more modern, electronic devices.

Gas detector could be single gas detectors and multi gas detector. It could be fixed, transportable or portable.

12.2 A **fixed detector** is permanently installed in a location to provide continuous monitoring of plant equipment. Often they cover a given range or area

12.3 **Transportable detectors** are not designed to be hand carried for long periods of time and are intended to be in place for hours or days. They can be used to monitor

an area while a fixed gas detector is undergoing
maintenance.

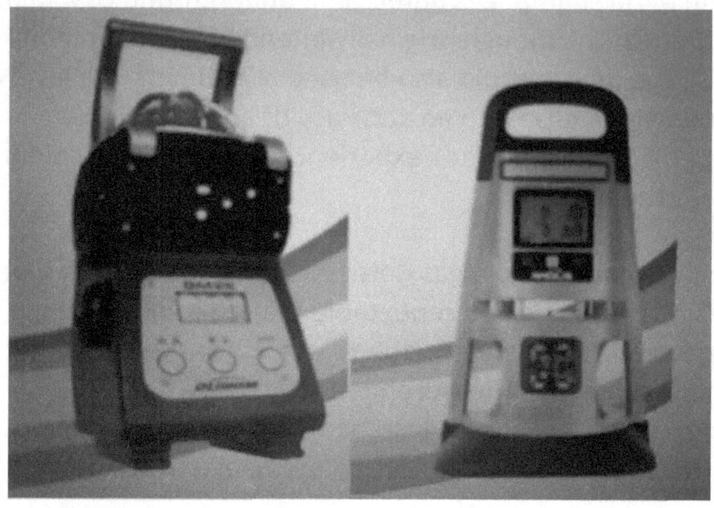

12.4 Portable gas detectors are small handheld
devices that could be used for testing atmosphere for
flammable and explosive gases. Portable detectors are
useful for tracing leaks of spot checks to give early warning
of the presence of flammable gases or vapour when work
is being carried out in a hazardous area.

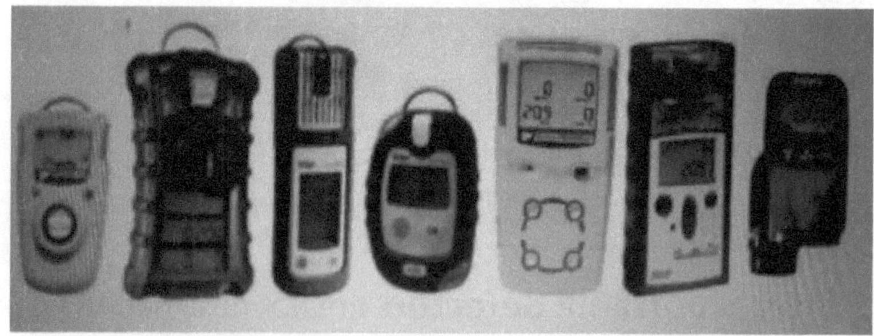

Portable gas detectors could be used **actively** or **passively**

12.4.1 Active Use:

Active use of a detector is where an operator carries the instrument around whilst monitoring. This may be in order to find leak, carry out spot checks, and conduct local area monitoring or to check the atmosphere for vessel entry.

12.4.2 Passive Use:

Passive use of a detector is where the instrument is positioned temporarily in one place to monitor the atmosphere. This temporary installation may be for a period of hours or days.

12.5 MODE OF MEASUREMENT

The unit of measurement is

%age volume ratio for oxygen.

%age volume ratio for Lower Explosive Limit (LEL) for flammable gas.

Parts per million (ppm) for toxic gases.

It is important that the user understands the significance of the units of measurement when setting alarm levels, etc.

CHAPTER THIRTEEN

TYPES OF DETECTORS

13.1   CATALYTIC DETECTOR:

Nevertheless, today's most commonly used device, the catalytic detector, is in some respects a modern development of the early flame safety lamp, since it also relies for its operation on the combustion of a gas and its conversion to carbon dioxide and water.

Nearly all modern, low-cost, combustible gas detection sensors are of the electro-catalytic type. They consist of a very small sensing element sometimes called a 'bead'. They are made of an electrically heated platinum wire coil, covered first with a ceramic base such as alumina and then with a final outer coating of palladium or rhodium catalyst dispersed in a substrate of thoria.

This type of sensor operates on the principle that when a combustible gas/air mixture passes over the hot catalyst surface, combustion occurs and the heat evolved increases the temperature of the 'bead'. This in turn alters the resistance of the platinum coil and can be measured by using the coil as a temperature thermometer in a standard electrical bridge circuit. The resistance change is then directly related to the gas concentration in the surrounding atmosphere and can be displayed on a meter or some similar indicating device.

The most common failure in catalytic sensors is performance degradation caused by exposure to certain poisons'. It is therefore essential that any gas monitoring system should not only be calibrated at the time of installation, but also checked regularly and re-calibrated as necessary. Checks must be made using an accurately calibrated standard gas mixture so that the zero and 'span' levels can be set correctly on the controller.

13.2   SEMICONDUCTOR SENSOR

Sensors made from semiconducting materials gained considerably in popularity during the late 1980's and at one time appeared to offer the possibility of a universal, low cost gas detector. In the same way as catalytic sensors, they operate by virtue of gas absorption at the surface of a heated oxide. In fact, this is a thin metal-oxide film (usually oxides of the transition metals or heavy metals, such as tin) deposited on a silicon slice by much the same process as is used in the manufacture of computer 'chips'. Absorption of the sample gas on the oxide surface, followed by catalytic oxidation, results in a change of electrical resistance of the oxide material and can be related to the sample gas concentration.

The surface of the sensor is heated to a constant temperature of about 200-250°C, to speed up the rate of reaction and to reduce the effects of ambient temperature changes.

13.3   THERMAL CONDUCTIVITY

This technique for detecting gas is suitable for the measurement of high (%V/V) concentrations of binary gas mixtures. It is mainly used for detecting gases with a thermal conductivity much greater than air e.g. Methane and Hydrogen. Gases with thermal conductivities close to air cannot be detected E.g. Ammonia and Carbon Monoxide. Gases with thermal conductivities less than air are more difficult to detect as water vapour can cause interference E.g. Carbon Dioxide and Butane. Mixtures of two gases in the absence of air can also be measured using this technique.

The heated sensing element is exposed to the sample and the reference element is enclosed in a sealed compartment. If the thermal conductivity of the sample gas is higher than that of the reference, then the temperature of the sensing element decreases. If the thermal conductivity of the sample gas is less than that of the reference then the temperature of the sample element increases. These temperature changes are proportional to the concentration of gas present at the sample element.

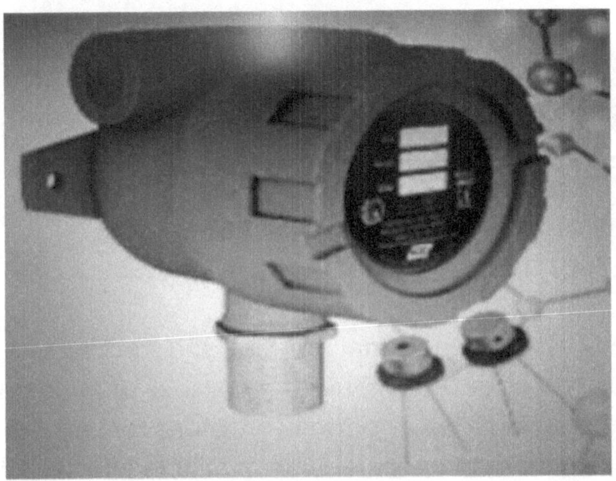

13.4   INFRARED GAS DETECTOR

Many combustible gases have absorption bands in the infrared region of the electromagnetic spectrum of light and the principle of infrared absorption has been used as a laboratory analytical tool for many years. Since the 1980's, however, electronic and optical advances have made it possible to design equipment of sufficiently low power and smaller size to make this technique available for industrial gas detection products as well.

These sensors have a number of important advantages over the catalytic type. They include a very fast speed of response (typically less than 10 seconds), low maintenance and greatly simplified checking, using the self-checking facility of modern micro-processor controlled equipment. They can also be designed to be unaffected by any known 'poisons', they are failsafe and they will operate successfully in inert atmospheres, and under a wide range of ambient temperature, pressure and humidity conditions.

This type of detector can only detect diatomic gas molecules and is therefore unsuitable for the detection of Hydrogen.

13.4.1 OPEN PATH FLAMMABLE INFRARED GAS DETECTOR

Traditionally, the conventional method of detecting gas leaks was by point detection, using a number of individual sensors to cover an area or perimeter. More recently, however, instruments have become available which make use of infrared and laser technology in the form of a broad beam (or open path) which can cover a distance of several hundred metres. Early open path designs were typically used to complement point detection, however the latest 3rd generation instruments are now often being used as the primary method of detection. Typical applications where they have had considerable success include FPSOs, loading/unloading terminals, pipelines, perimeter monitoring, off-shore platforms and LNG (Liquid Natural Gas) storage areas.

Open path detectors actually measure the total number of gas molecules (i.e. the quantity of gas) within the beam. This value is different to the usual concentration of gas given at a single point and is therefore expressed in terms of LEL meters.

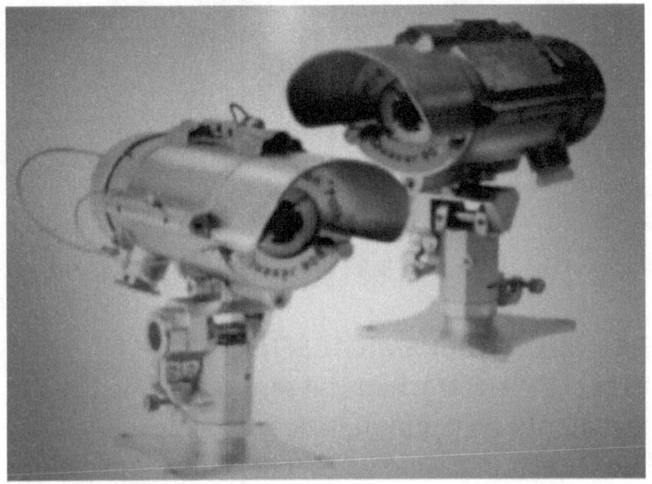

13.4.2 OPEN PATH TOXIC INFRARED GAS DETECTOR

With the availability of reliable solid state laser diode sources in the near infrared region and also the increase in processing power afforded by the latest generation of digital signal processors, it is now feasible to consider the production of a new generation of gas detector for the reliable detection of toxic gases by optical means.

Optical open path and point detection of flammable gas is now well established and has been widely accepted in the Petrochemical industry where they have proved to be a viable and reliable measurement technology.

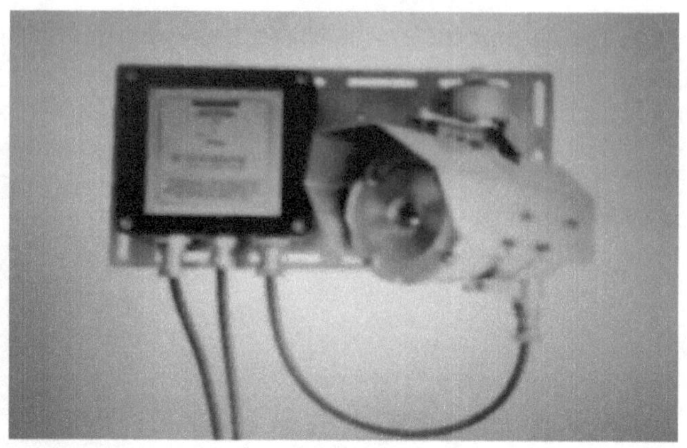

13.5   ELECTROCHEMICAL SENSOR

Gas specific electrochemical sensors can be used to detect the majority of common toxic gases, including CO, H2S, Cl2, SO2 etc. in a wide variety of safety applications. Electrochemical sensors are compact, require very little power, exhibit excellent linearity and repeatability and generally have a long life span, typically one to three years. Response times, denoted as T90, i.e. time to reach 90% of the final response, are typically 30-60 seconds and minimum detection limits range from 0.02 to 50ppm depending upon target gas type.

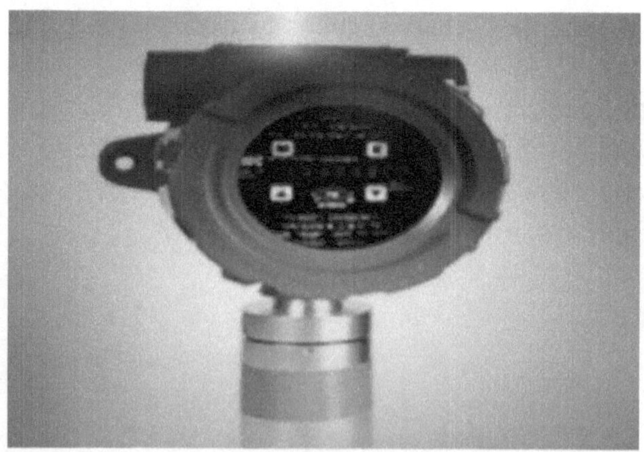

CHAPTER FOURTEEN

TOXIC GAS HAZARDS

Some gases are poisonous and can be dangerous to life at very low concentrations. Some toxic gases have strong smells like the distinctive 'rotten eggs' smell of H_2S. The measurements most often used for the concentration of toxic gases are parts per million (ppm) and parts per billion (ppb). For example 1ppm would be equivalent to a room filled with a total of 1 million balls and 1 of those balls being red. The red ball would represent 1ppm.

More people die from toxic gas exposure than from explosions caused by the ignition of flammable gas. (It should be noted that there is a large group of gases which are both combustible and toxic, so that even detectors of toxic gases sometimes have to carry hazardous area approval). The main reason for treating flammable and toxic gases separately is that the hazards and regulations involved and the types of sensor required are different.

With toxic substances, (apart from the obvious environmental problems) the main concern is the effect on workers of exposure to even at very low concentrations, which could be inhaled, ingested, or absorbed through the skin. Since adverse effects can often result from additive, long-term exposure, it is important not only to measure the concentration of gas, but also the total time of exposure.

Concern about concentrations of toxic substances in the workplace focus on both organic and inorganic compounds, including the effects they could have on the health and safety of employees, the possible

39

contamination of a manufactured end-product and also the subsequent disruption of normal working activities.

14.1 ASPHYXIANT (OXYGEN DEFICIENCY) HAZARD

We all need to breathe the oxygen (O_2) in air to live. Air is made up of several different gases including oxygen. Normal ambient air contains an oxygen concentration of 20.9% v/v. When the oxygen level dips below 19.5% v/v, the air is considered oxygen deficient. Oxygen concentrations below 16% v/v are considered unsafe for humans.

14.2 OXYGEN ENRICHMENT

It is often forgotten that oxygen enrichment can also cause a risk. At increased oxygen O_2 levels the flammability of materials and gases increases. At levels of 24% items such as clothing can spontaneously combust.
Increasing the level of O_2 past the normal 20.9% which is present in the atmosphere will increase the flammability of any combustible matter.

This is because there are three elements a fire needs to ignite, which are fuel, heat and an oxidising agent (usually O_2).

Materials such as aluminium, steel and stainless steel are hard to burn in normal atmospheric conditions, but wood can easily burn due to its ignition temperature being much lower than steel.

By raising the concentration of O_2 in the atmosphere, this causes the auto-ignition temperature of materials to decrease and their flammability range increases.

Materials that cannot be ignited in normal air may burn in an Oxygen O_2 enriched environment, while materials that do burn in air will burn hotter and faster.

Even clothes can trap and hold enriched O_2 within the weave of the fabric and if they are near an ignition source, they can easily catch fire.

The Occupational Safety and Health Administration (OSHA) determines the acceptable levels of the Oxygen are between 19.5% and 23.5%.

Oxygen is colourless, odourless and tasteless, making it hard to detect the presence of an oxygen enriched atmosphere.

If you store or operate with high levels of Oxygen you need to monitor the atmosphere, as a leak of enriched O_2 could prove to be a fire risk.

14.3 HYDROGEN SULPHIDE

Hydrogen sulphide (H_2S) is a colourless gas with a characteristic odour of rotten eggs which being denser than air may pool in low areas in still conditions. Hydrogen sulphide occurs naturally in some environments such as sulphur springs, swamps and salt marshes, and is often associated with the decomposition of organic material. Human activities and industries that may produce hydrogen sulphide include:

- Sewage treatment plants
- Tanneries
- Piggeries
- Manure handling operations.

Hydrogen sulphide has also been found to contaminate bore water and surface water bodies, usually at low levels, due to bacteria which convert sulphur materials into hydrogen sulphide.
This may especially be the case where acid sulphate soils have been disturbed.

14.3.1 Exposure to hydrogen sulphide

People are normally exposed to hydrogen sulphide in air by breathing it in or by skin/eye contact.
Any absorbed hydrogen sulphide does not accumulate in the body as it is rapidly metabolised in the liver and excreted in the urine.
Hydrogen sulphide usually breaks down in air in about 3 days and is dispersed by wind.
Therefore exposure is only likely to continue if there is an ongoing source.

14.3.2 How can hydrogen sulphide affect health?

Hydrogen sulphide has a characteristic rotten egg smell which can be detected at very low levels, well below those that are known to cause health effects.
Smelling hydrogen sulphide does not mean that it will harm your health.
The smell can cause worry, anxiety and resentment.
Repeated odour events may culminate in real symptoms such as headache, fatigue and nausea. Although these are not direct health effects they are undesirable.
Real human impacts from hydrogen sulphide are not likely until air levels reach at least 2 ppm for 30 minutes.
At this point sensitive groups such as some asthmatics may respond with some minor irritative changes in their bronchial capacity.

The lowest level for adverse health effects is at least 500 times the odour detection limit.

At this level, irritation of the mucous membranes of the eye can occur.

The impacts and health effects of exposure to the levels of hydrogen sulphide that may be possible in the environment are shown in the table below.

Level in air (ppm)	Impacts and health effects
0.008	Odour threshold (with some individual variability)
0.008	Increasing possibility of annoyance and headache, nausea, fatigue
2	Bronchial restriction in some asthmatics
4	Increased eye complaints
5-10	Minor metabolic effects
20	Neurological effects including memory loss and dizziness

14.3.3 How are children affected?

It is not clear whether children are more sensitive than adults to hydrogen sulphide although they are likely to show the same types of effects.

However, care should be taken since children are lower to the ground where hydrogen sulphide may be more concentrated and active children may breathe in more of the gas.

14.3.4 Exposure guidelines for hydrogen sulphide.

Limit (ppm)	Averaging timeframe
2	30 minutes
0.1	24 hours
0.014	90 days

Averaging timeframe is the time over which the measured level of hydrogen sulphide in air is averaged and relates to potential short or possibly longer term effects. The 2 ppm limit value is associated with bronchial effects in some sensitive asthmatics and so should not be exceeded. The other limit values have safety margins built into them and so an exceedance does not necessarily mean a health consequence.

14.3.5 Levels in water

The bore water or any water that contains more than 0.05 mg/L of hydrogen sulphide, should be assessed for suitability for human use.

This is based on protecting the aesthetic quality of the water (smell and taste) and is not related to health.

Drinking or immersion in water above this level of contamination normally would be unpleasant.

At high concentrations of hydrogen sulphide in water, emissions of the gas may pose a respiratory risk to health under unfavourable conditions such as prolonged large scale irrigation close to residences.

14.3.6 How can I reduce exposure to hydrogen sulphide?

If the smell of hydrogen sulphide is strong or you are concerned about its impacts on your amenity or health, you can reduce your exposure by:

- Avoiding areas that are known sources of hydrogen sulphide.
- Keeping windows closed when the odour outdoors is noticeable and opening doors and windows once the outdoor odour has subsided.
- Not exercising outdoors when the smell is present, particularly if your breathing rate increases.
- If the hydrogen sulphide is being generated by human activities then appropriate management of those activities may help address the problem at source.
- When bore water is contaminated with hydrogen sulphide it is sometimes possible to treat the bore with an agent which removes iron from the water and therefore interferes with bacterial activity which happens to generate the gas. Water treatment companies can advise on suitable agents. Use of hydrogen sulphide impacted water for irrigation

purposes has the potential to release considerable amounts of gas, as mentioned above.

14.3.7 Methods for reducing odour impacts include:

- Decreasing the quantity of water used.
- Using drippers or delivery devices which are low to the ground and have large droplet size.
- Watering when there is sufficient wind to disperse the odour.
- Watering at night when there are fewer people around, if wind is sufficient

14.4 CARBON MONOXIDE POISONING

Carbon monoxide, or Carbon Monoxide, is a toxic gas that you cannot see or smell. Carbon Monoxide is given off whenever fuel or other carbon-based materials are burned. Carbon Monoxide usually comes from sources in or near your home that are not properly maintained or vented.

Carbon monoxide poisoning occurs when carbon monoxide builds up in your bloodstream. When too much carbon monoxide is in the air, your body replaces the oxygen in your red blood cells with carbon monoxide. This can lead to serious tissue damage, or even death.

Carbon monoxide is a colourless, odourless, tasteless gas produced by burning gasoline, wood, propane, charcoal or other fuel. Improperly ventilated appliances and engines, particularly in a tightly sealed or enclosed space, may allow carbon monoxide to accumulate to dangerous levels.

If you think you or someone you're with may have carbon monoxide poisoning, get into fresh air and seek emergency medical care.

You may be exposed to unsafe levels of carbon monoxide by:

- Using poorly maintained or unvented heating equipment;
- Improperly vented natural gas appliances like stoves or water heaters;
- Running vehicles in garages or other enclosed spaces;
- Using a gas stove, grill, or oven to heat the home;
- House or building fires;
- Clogged chimneys or blocked heating exhaust vents;
- Running generators or gas-powered tools indoors or outside near windows, doors, or vents;
- Cooking with a charcoal or gas grill inside the home or other enclosure;
- Using a propane camp stove, heater, or light inside a tent; and
- Being near boat engine exhaust outlets.

14.4.1 Symptoms of Carbon Monoxide Poisoning

Signs and symptoms of carbon monoxide poisoning may include:

- Dull headache.
- Weakness.
- Dizziness.

- Nausea or vomiting.
- Shortness of breath.
- Confusion.
- Blurred vision.
- Loss of consciousness

Carbon monoxide poisoning can be particularly dangerous for people who are sleeping or intoxicated. People may have irreversible brain damage or even die before anyone realizes there is a problem.

The warning signs of carbon monoxide poisoning can be subtle. But the condition is a life-threatening medical emergency. If you think you or someone has carbon monoxide poisoning, get into fresh air and seek emergency medical care.

14.4.2 Causes of Carbon Monoxide

Carbon monoxide poisoning is caused by inhaling combustion fumes. When too much carbon monoxide is in the air you are breathing, your body replaces the oxygen in your red blood cells with carbon monoxide. This prevents oxygen from reaching your tissues and organs.

Various fuel-burning appliances and engines produce carbon monoxide. The amount of carbon monoxide produced by these sources usually is not cause for concern. But if they are used in a closed or partially closed space example cooking with a charcoal grill indoors, the carbon monoxide can build to dangerous levels. Smoke inhalation during a fire also can cause carbon monoxide poisoning.

14.4.3 Who is at risk of Carbon Monoxide

Exposure to carbon monoxide may be particularly dangerous for:

- **Unborn babies.** Foetal blood cells take up carbon monoxide more readily than adult blood cells do. This makes unborn babies more susceptible to harm from carbon monoxide poisoning.
- **Children.** Young children take breaths more frequently than adults do, which may make them more susceptible to carbon monoxide poisoning.
- **Older adults.** Older people who experience carbon monoxide poisoning may be more likely to develop brain damage.
- **People who have chronic heart disease.** People with a history of anaemia and breathing problems also are more likely to get sick from exposure to carbon monoxide.

14.4.4 Complications of Carbon Monoxide

Depending on the degree and length of exposure, carbon monoxide poisoning can cause:

- Permanent brain damage
- Damage to your heart, possibly leading to life-threatening cardiac complications
- Foetal death or miscarriage
- Death

14.4.5 Prevention of Carbon Monoxide

Simple precautions can help prevent carbon monoxide poisoning:

- **Install carbon monoxide detectors.** Put one in the hallway near each sleeping area in your house. Check the batteries every time you check your smoke detector batteries. If the alarm sounds, leave the house for a safe place with fresh air.
- **Open the garage door before starting your car.** Never leave your car running in your garage. Be particularly cautious if you have an attached garage. Leaving your car running in a space attached to the rest of your house is never safe, even with the garage door open.

- **Use gas appliances as recommended.** Never use a gas stove or oven to heat your home. Use portable gas camp stoves outdoors only. Use fuel-burning space heaters only when someone is awake to monitor them and doors or windows are open to provide fresh air. Don't run a generator in an enclosed space, such as the basement or garage.

- **Keep your fuel-burning appliances and engines properly vented.** These include: Space heaters, Furnaces, Charcoal grills, Cooking ranges, Water heaters, Fireplaces, Portable generators, Wood-burning stoves and Car and truck engines

- **If you have a fireplace, keep it in good repair.** Clean
  your fireplace chimney and flue regularly

- **Keep vents and chimneys unblocked during
  remodelling.** Check that they aren't covered by tarps
  or debris.

- **Make repairs before returning to the site of an
  incident.** If carbon monoxide poisoning has occurred
  in your home, it's critical to find and repair the
  source of the carbon monoxide before you stay there
  again. Contact your local fire department or utility
  company for help.

- **Use caution when working with solvents in a closed
  area.** Methylene chloride, a solvent commonly found
  in paint and varnish removers, can break down
  (metabolize) into carbon monoxide when inhaled.
  Exposure to methylene chloride can cause carbon
  monoxide poisoning.

  When working with solvents at home, use them only
  outdoors or in well-ventilated areas. Carefully read
  the instructions and follow the safety precautions on
  the label

CHAPTER FIFTEEN

TYPICAL AREAS THAT REQUIRE GAS DETECTION

There are many different applications for flammable, toxic and oxygen gas detection. Industrial processes increasingly involve the use and manufacture of highly dangerous substances, particularly toxic and combustible gases. Inevitably, occasional escapes of gas occur, which create a potential hazard to the industrial plant, its employees and people living nearby. Worldwide incidents involving asphyxiation, explosions and loss of life, are a constant reminder of this problem.

In most industries, one of the key parts of the safety plan for reducing the risks to personnel and plant is the use of early warning devices such as gas detectors. These can help to provide more time in which to take remedial or protective action. They can also be used as part of a total integrated monitoring and safety system for an industrial plant.

15.1   OIL & GAS

The oil and gas industry covers a large number of upstream activities from the on and offshore exploration and production of oil and gas to its transportation, storage and refining. The large amount of highly flammable Hydrocarbon gases involved are a serious explosive risk and additionally toxic gases such as Hydrogen Sulphide are often present.

Typical Applications:

- Exploration- Drilling Rigs
- Production Platforms
- Onshore oil and gas terminals

- Refineries

Typical Gases:

Flammable: Hydrocarbon gases
Toxic: Hydrogen Sulphide, Carbon Monoxide

15.2 SEMICONDUCTOR MANUFACTURING

Manufacturing semiconductor materials involves the use of highly toxic substances and flammable gas. Phosphorus, arsenic, boron and gallium are commonly used as doping agents. Hydrogen is used both as a reactant and a reducing atmosphere carrier gas.

Typical Applications:

- Wafer reactor
- Wafer dryers
- Gas Cabinets
- Chemical Vapour Deposition

Typical Gases:

Flammable: Flammable: Hydrogen, Isopropyl Alcohol, Methane
Toxic: HCl, AsH3, BCl3, PH3, CO, HF, O3, H2Cl2Si, TEOS, C4F6, C5F8, GeH4, NH3, NO2 and O2 Deficiency.

15.3 CHEMICAL PLANTS

Probably one of the largest users of gas detection equipment are Chemical Plants. They often use a wide range of both flammable and toxic gases in their manufacturing processes or create them as by-products of the processes.

Typical Applications:

- Raw material storage
- Process areas
- Laboratories
- Pump rows

- Compressor stations
- Loading/unloading areas

Typical Gases:

Flammable: General Hydrocarbons
Toxic: Hydrogen Sulphide, Hydrogen Fluoride and Ammonia

15.4   POWER STATIONS

Traditionally coal and oil have been used as the main fuel for Power Stations.

In Europe and the US most are being converted to natural gas.

Typical Applications:

- Around the boiler pipe work and burners
- In and around turbine packages
- In coal silos and conveyor belts in older coal/oil fired stations

Typical Gases:

Flammable: Natural Gas, Hydrogen
Toxic: Carbon Monoxide, SOx, NOx and Oxygen deficiency.

15.5   WASTE WATER TREATMENT PLANTS

Waste Water Treatment Plants are a familiar site around many cities and towns.

Sewage naturally gives off both Methane and H2S. The 'rotten eggs' smell of H2S can often be noticed as the nose can detect it at less than 0.1ppm.

Typical Applications:

- Digesters
- Plant sumps
- H2S Scrubbers
- Pumps

Typical Gases:
Flammable: Methane, Solvent vapours
Toxic: Hydrogen Sulphide, Carbon Dioxide, Chlorine, Sulphur Dioxide, and Ozone.

15.6   BOILER ROOMS

Boiler Rooms come in all shapes and sizes. Small buildings may have a single boiler whereas larger buildings often have large boiler rooms housing several large boilers.
Typical Applications:
- Flammable gas leaks from the incoming gas
- Leaks from the boiler and surrounding gas piping
- Carbon Monoxide given off badly maintained boiler

Typical Gases:
Flammable: Methane
Toxic: Carbon Monoxide

15.7   HOSPITALS

Hospitals may use many different flammable and toxic substances, particularly in their laboratories. Additionally, many are very large and have onsite utility supplies and backup power stations.
Typical Applications:
- Laboratories
- Refrigeration plants
- Boiler rooms

Typical Gases:
Flammable: Methane, Hydrogen
Toxic: Carbon Monoxide, Chlorine, Ammonia, Ethylene oxide and Oxygen deficiency

15.8   TUNNELS/CAR PARKS

Car Tunnels and enclosed Car Parks need to be monitored for the toxic gases from exhaust fumes. Modern tunnels and car parks use this monitoring to control the ventilation fans. Tunnels may also need to be monitored for the build-up of natural gas.

Typical Applications:

- Car tunnels
- Underground and enclosed car parks
- Access tunnels
- Ventilation control

Typical Gases:

Flammable: Methane (natural gas), LPG, LNG, Petrol Vapour.

Toxic: Carbon Monoxide, Nitrogen Dioxide

CHAPTER SIXTEEN

WORKPLACE EXPOSURE LIMIT

A workplace **exposure limit** is an upper limit acceptable concentration of a hazardous substance in workplace air for a particular material or class of materials. It is typically set by competent national authorities and enforced by legislation to protect occupational safety and health. It is an important tool in risk assessment and in the management of activities involving handling of dangerous substances.

The exposure routes include:

- By breathing fume, dust, gas or mist
- By skin contact
- By injection into the skin
- By swallowing

The Workplace Exposure Limit have both 8 hour and 15 minutes exposure limits expressed as airborne concentrations averaged over a specified period of time referred to as a Time Weighted average (TWA). Two time periods are used: Long term (8 Hour) and Short term (15 minutes).

16.1 Time Weighted Average (TWA): Is a Toxic gas Limits related to concentration & time.

Time weighted average is the maximum allowable concentration of a toxic substance a worker can be exposed to over a working period of 8 hour workday and 40-hour work week

16.2 Short Term Exposure Limit (STEL): This is the maximum allowable concentration of a toxic substance a worker can be exposed to over a working period of 15 minutes.

16.3 Long Term Exposure Limit (LTEL)/TWA: It is the maximum allowable concentration of a toxic substance a worker can be exposed to over a working period of 8-hour workday and a 40-hour workweek.

16.4 Permissible Exposure Limit (PEL): Is the maximum amount/concentration of a chemical that a worker may be exposed to under OSHA Regulation.

16.5 PEL-TWA: The average amount of a chemical that a worker can be exposed to 8-hours a day, 5 days a week.

Substance	8 Hour Exposure Limit (ppm)	15 Minutes Exposure Limit (ppm)
Acetone	500	1500
Ammonia	25	35
n-Butane	600	750
Carbon Dioxide	5000	1500
Carbon Monoxide	30	200
Chlorine	0.5	1
Hydrogen Sulphide	5	10

CHAPTER SEVENTEEN

TEMPERATURE OF HAZARDOUS MATERIAL

As well as considering the protection against electrical arcs and sparks igniting a flammable atmosphere, consideration needs to be given to the surface temperature of equipment. Most electrical apparatus dissipates some heat. Flammable materials are categorized according to their ignition temperature.

17.1 AUTO-IGNITION TEMPERATURE:

The **auto ignition temperature** or **kindling point** of a substance is the lowest temperature at which it spontaneously ignites in normal atmosphere without an external source of ignition, such as a flame or spark. This temperature is required to supply the activation energy needed for combustion. The temperature at which a chemical ignites decreases as the pressure or oxygen concentration increases. It is usually applied to a combustible fuel mixture.

Substance	Auto-ignition
Barium	550 °C (1,022 °F)
Bismuth	735 °C (1,355 °F)
Butane	405 °C (761 °F)
Calcium	790 °C (1,450 °F)
Carbon disulphide	90 °C (194 °F)
Diesel or Jet A-1	210 °C (410 °F)

Substance	Auto-ignition
Diethyl ether	160 °C (320 °F)
Ethanol	365 °C (689 °F)
Gasoline(Petrol)	247–280 °C (477–536 °F)
Hydrogen	536 °C (997 °F)
Iron	1,315 °C (2,399 °F)
Lead	850 °C (1,560 °F)
Leather/Parchment	200–212 °C (392–414 °F)
Magnesium	635 °C (1,175 °F)
Magnesium	473 °C (883 °F)
Molybdenum	780 °C (1,440 °F)
Paper	218–246 °C (424–475 °F)
Phosphorus, white	34 °C (93 °F)
Silane	21 °C (70 °F)
Strontium	1,075 °C (1,967 °F)
Tin	940 °C (1,720 °F)
Triethylborane	–20 °C (–4 °F)

17.2 FLASH POINT

The **flash point** of a volatile material is the lowest temperature at which vapours of the material will ignite, when given an ignition source.

The flash point is sometimes confused with the auto-ignition temperature, the temperature that results in spontaneous auto-ignition. The fire point is the lowest temperature at which vapours of the material will keep burning after the ignition source is removed. The fire point is higher than the **flash point**, because at the flash point more vapour may not be produced rapidly enough to sustain combustion. Either flash point or fire point depends directly on the ignition source temperature, but ignition source temperature is far higher than either the flash or fire point.

The flash point is a descriptive characteristic that is used to distinguish between flammable fuels, such as petrol, and combustible fuels, such as diesel.

Fuels which have a flash point less than 37.8 °C (100.0 °F) are called flammable, whereas fuels having a flash point above that temperature are called combustible.

All liquids have a specific vapour pressure, which is a function of that liquid's temperature. As temperature increases, vapour pressure increases. As vapour pressure increases, the concentration of vapour of a flammable or combustible liquid in the air increases. Hence, temperature determines the concentration of vapour of the flammable liquid in the air. A certain concentration of a flammable or combustible vapour is necessary to sustain combustion in air.

There are two basic types of flash point measurement: **open cup** and **closed cup.**

In **open cup** devices, the sample is contained in an open cup which is heated and, at intervals, a flame brought over the surface. The measured flash point will actually vary with the height of the flame above the liquid surface and, at sufficient height, the measured flash point temperature will coincide with the fire point. There are two types of closed cup testers: non-equilibrial, - where the vapours above the liquid are not in temperature equilibrium with the liquid, and equilibrial, such as Small Scale (commonly known as Setaflash), where the vapours are deemed to be in temperature equilibrium with the liquid. In both these types, the cups are sealed with a lid through which the ignition source can be introduced. Closed cup testers normally give lower values for the flash point than open cup (typically 5–10 °C or 9–18 °F lower) and are a better approximation to the temperature at which the vapour pressure reaches the lower flammable limit.

The flash point is an empirical measurement rather than a fundamental physical parameter. The measured value will vary with equipment and test protocol variations, including temperature ramp rate (in automated testers), time allowed for the sample to equilibrate, sample volume and whether the sample is stirred.

Fuel	Flash point	Auto-ignition temperature
Ethanol (70%)	16.6 °C (61.9 °F)	363 °C (685 °F)
Petrol	−43 °C (−45 °F)	280 °C (536 °F)
Diesel	>52 °C (126 °F)	210 °C (410 °F)
Jet Fuel	>38 °C (100 °F)	210 °C (410 °F)
Kerosene	>38–72 °C (100–162 °F)	220 °C (428 °F)
Vegetable oil	327 °C (621 °F)	424 °C (795 °F)
Biodiesel	>130 °C (266 °F)	

17.3 TEMPERATURE CLASSES

There are six temperature classes as defined below:

T-Class	Hazards which will not ignite at temperatures below:
T1	450°C
T2	300°C
T3	200°C
T4	135°C
T5	100°C
T6	85°C

17.3.1 TEMPERATURE CLASSES EXPLAINED

The bigger the T-number the lower is the temperature.
The Temperature classification will be marked on items of
equipment. If the hazardous area in which you are
installing equipment has gases or vapours with a low auto-
ignition temperature then you will need equipment with a
bigger T-Number so as to ensure that any hot surfaces on
the equipment will not ignite the hazard.

For example, if a hazard has an auto-ignition temperature
of 180°C, then it would be safe to use equipment which is
marked T6 or T5 or T4(refer to temperature classes table
above). It would not be safe to use equipment marked T3
or T2 or T1 (**because temperature class of T3, T2 & T1 is
lower than the auto-ignition temperature of hazard, that
means before the hazard gets to its own auto-ignition
temperature, the equipment has started to release
sparks and heat capable to ignite the hazard)** as this

equipment could exhibit surface temperatures which are hot enough to ignite the hazardous atmosphere.

Don't forget that, unless the certification documents state otherwise *(in which case there will be an addition to the T-Classification code on the equipment label such as T4 (60°C Amb))* the equipment is only certified in ambient temperatures up to 40°C. If exposed to higher temperatures there are two possible dangers. First the stated T-Class temperature may be exceeded and secondly safety components within the equipment could fail to an unsafe condition. If you expect equipment to be subjected to temperatures above 40°C (such as in direct sunshine or in a roof space) you should install equipment which is certified for a higher ambient temperature.

CHAPTER EIGHTEEN

TYPES OF PROTECTION TO MAKE EQUIPMENT SUITABLE FOR HAZARDOUS AREA

Electrical apparatus for use in hazardous areas needs to be designed and constructed in such a way that it will not provide a source of ignition. There are ten recognized types of protection for hazardous area electrical apparatus. Each type of protection achieves its safety from ignition in different ways and not all are equally safe. In addition to the equipment being suitable for the Gas Group and the Temperature Class required, the type of protection must be suitable for the zone in which it is to be installed. The different types of protection and the zones for which they are suitable are as follows:

Equipment Code	Description	Suitable for zones...
Ex ia	Intrinsic safety 'ia'	0, 1, 2
Ex ib	Intrinsic safety 'ib'	1,2
Ex ic	Intrinsic Safety 'ic'	2
Ex d	Flameproof protection	1,2
Ex p	Purge/pressurized protection	1,2
Ex px	Purge/pressurized protection 'px'	1,2
Ex py	Purge/pressurized protection 'py'	1,2
Ex pz	Purge/pressurized protection 'pz'	2
Ex e	Increased safety	1,2
Ex m	Encapsulation	1,2
Ex ma	Encapsulation	0,1,2
Ex mb	Encapsulation	1.2
Ex o	Oil immersion	1,2
Ex q	Sand / powder (quartz) filling	1,2

Ex n	Type - n protection	2
Ex s	Special protection	Normally 1 and 2

Equipment complying with European (CENELEC) standards will frequently bear the code EEx (as opposed to Ex) But note that the use of EEx is being phased out for equipment designed and certified to the latest editions of the European Standards.

CHAPTER NINETEEN

HAZARDOUS EQUIPMENT MAKINGS

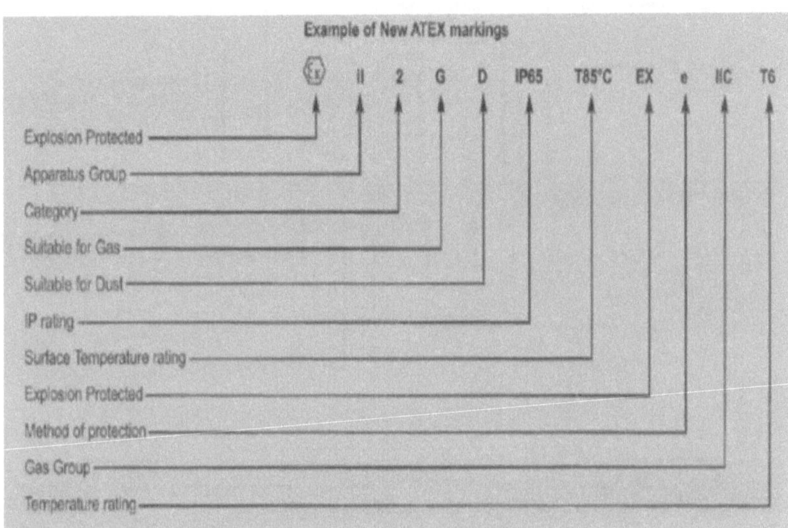

ATEX Symbols

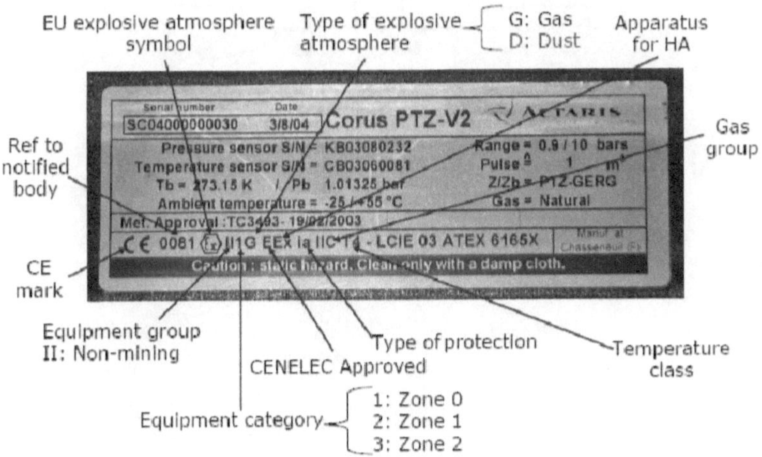

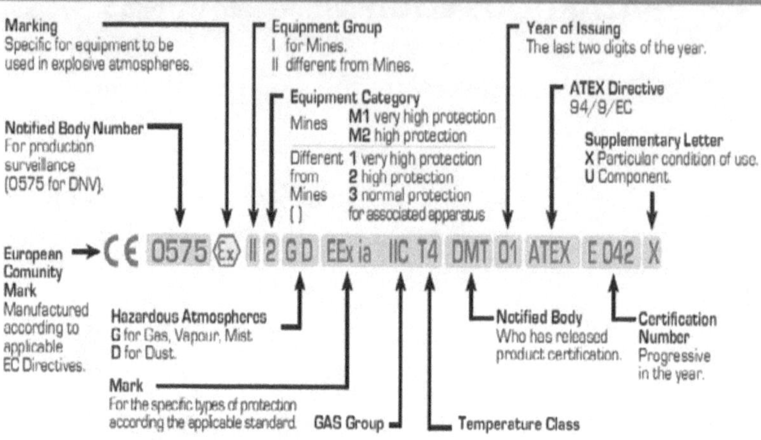

MARKING for NORTH AMERICA according NEC / CEC

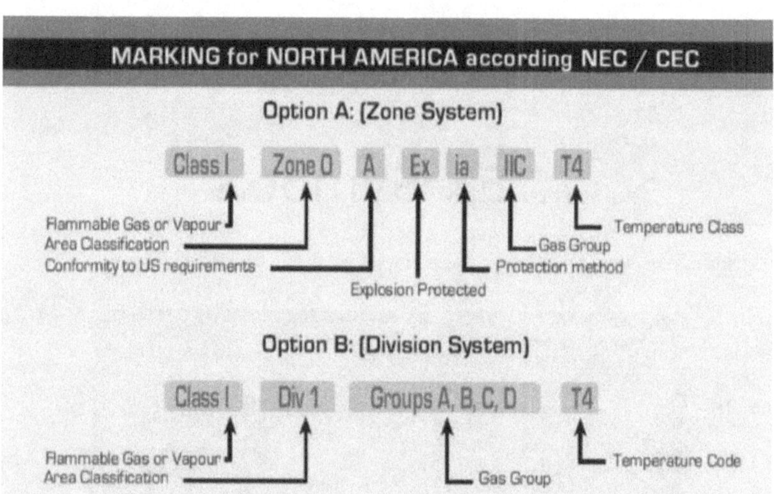

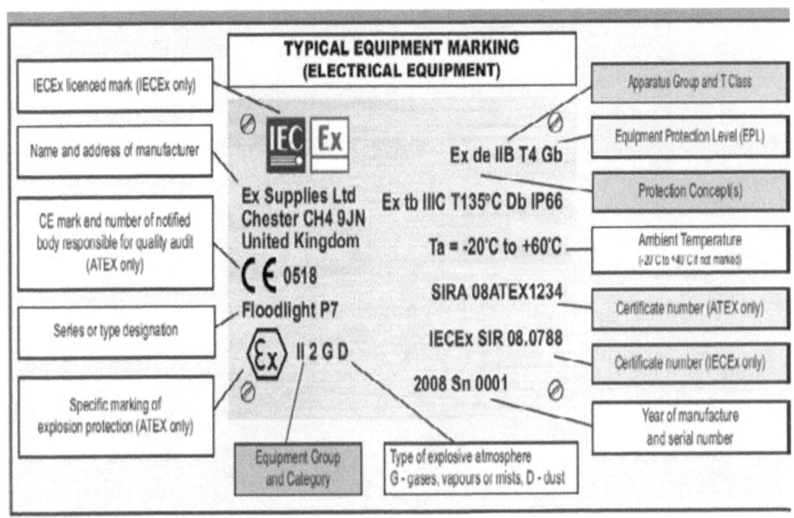

TYPICAL EQUIPMENT MARKING
(ELECTRICAL EQUIPMENT)
IECEx licenced mark (IECEx only)
Name and address of manufacturer
CE mark and number of notified body responsible for quality audit (ATEX only)
Series or type designation
Specific marking of explosion protection (ATEX only)
Equipment Group and Category
Type of explosive atmosphere
G - gases, vapours or mists, D - dust
IEC Ex
Ex Supplies Ltd
Chester CH4 9JN
United Kingdom
CE 0518
Floodlight P7
Ex II 2 G D
Ex de IIB T4 Gb
Ex tb IIIC T135°C Db IP66
Ta = -20°C to +60°C
SIRA 08ATEX1234
IECEx SIR 08.0788
2008 Sn 0001
Apparatus Group and T Class
Equipment Protection Level (EPL)
Protection Concept(s)
Ambient Temperature
(-20°C to +40°C if not marked)
Certificate number (ATEX only)
Certificate number (IECEx only)
Year of manufacture
and serial number

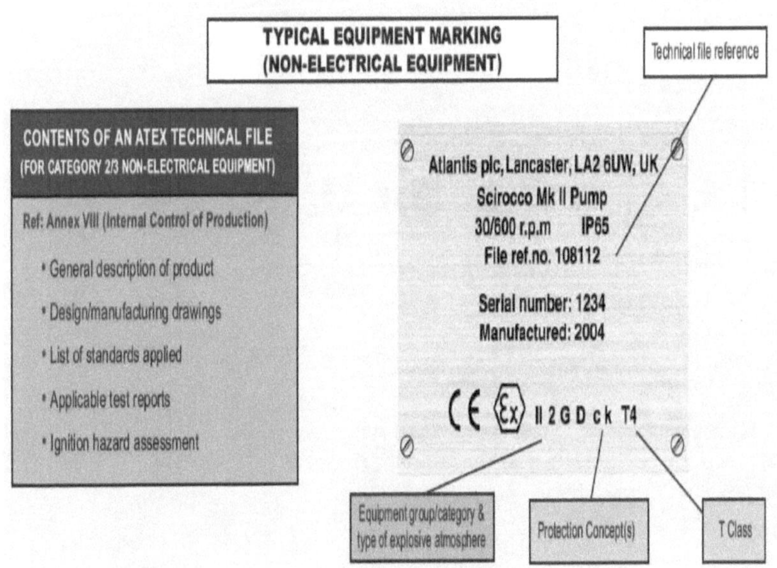

TYPICAL EQUIPMENT MARKING
(NON-ELECTRICAL EQUIPMENT)
Technical file reference
CONTENTS OF AN ATEX TECHNICAL FILE
(FOR CATEGORY 2/3 NON-ELECTRICAL EQUIPMENT)
Ref: Annex VIII (Internal Control of Production)
• General description of product
• Design/manufacturing drawings
• List of standards applied
• Applicable test reports
• Ignition hazard assessment
Atlantis plc, Lancaster, LA2 6UW, UK
Scirocco Mk II Pump
30/600 r.p.m   IP65
File ref.no. 108112
Serial number: 1234
Manufactured: 2004
CE Ex II 2 G D c k T4
Equipment group/category &
type of explosive atmosphere
Protection Concept(s)
T Class

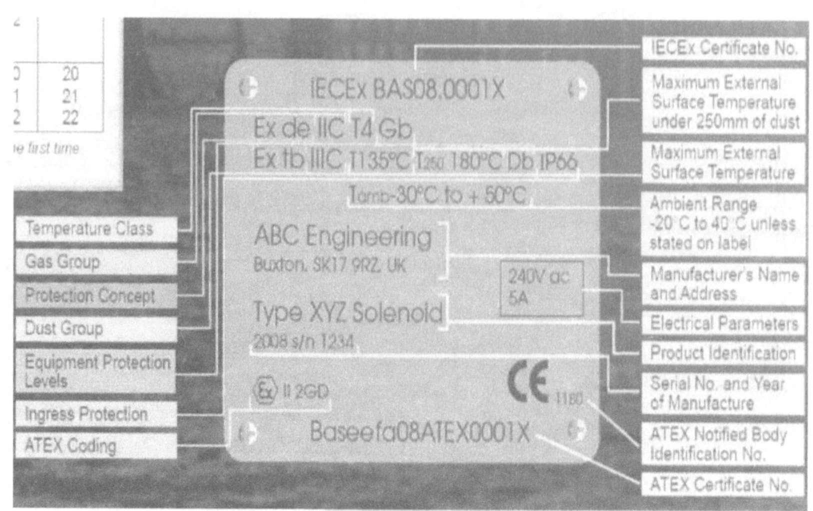
IECEx Certificate No.
Maximum External Surface Temperature under 250mm of dust
Maximum External Surface Temperature
Ambient Range -20°C to 40°C unless stated on label
Manufacturer's Name and Address
Electrical Parameters
Product Identification
Serial No. and Year of Manufacture
ATEX Notified Body Identification No.
ATEX Certificate No.
Temperature Class
Gas Group
Protection Concept
Dust Group
Equipment Protection Levels
Ingress Protection
ATEX Coding
IECEx BAS08.0001X
Ex de IIC T4 Gb
Ex tb IIIC T135°C T250 180°C Db IP66
Tamb-30°C to + 50°C
ABC Engineering
Buxton, SK17 9RZ, UK
Type XYZ Solenoid
2008 s/n 1234
240V ac 5A
Ex II 2GD
CE 1180
Baseefa08ATEX0001X

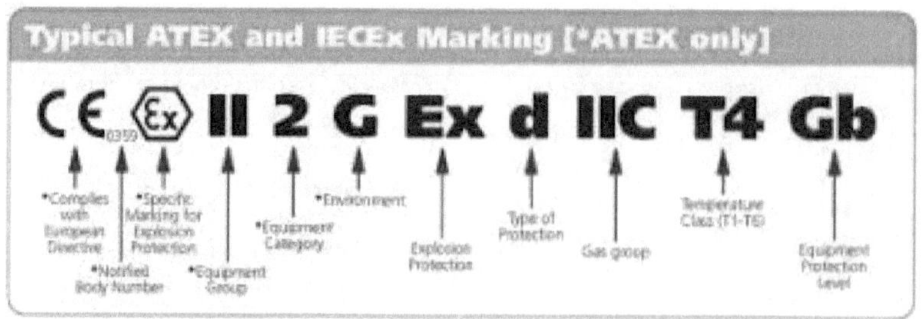
Typical ATEX and IECEx Marking [*ATEX only]
CE 0359 Ex II 2 G Ex d IIC T4 Gb
*Complies with European Directive
*Notified Body Number
*Specific Marking for Explosion Protection
*Equipment Group
*Equipment Category
*Environment
Explosion Protection
Type of Protection
Gas group
Temperature Class (T1-T6)
Equipment Protection Level

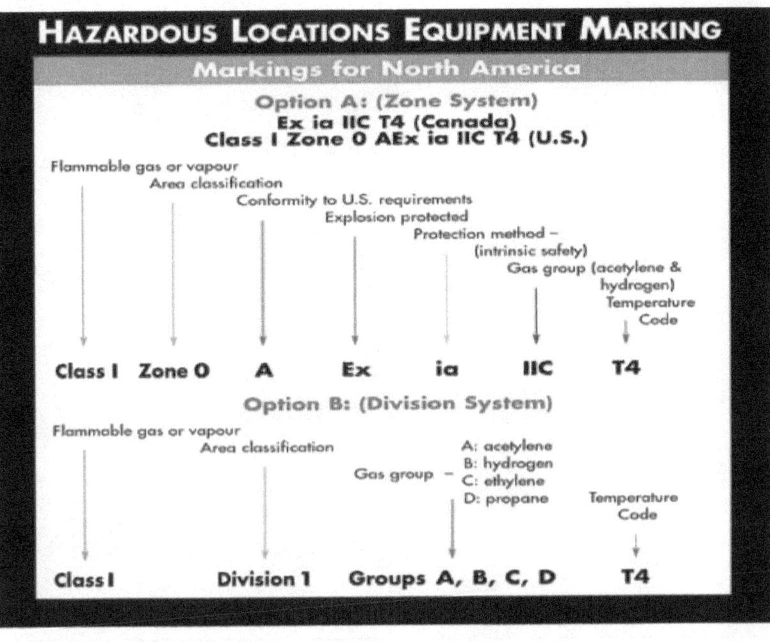

HAZARDOUS LOCATIONS EQUIPMENT MARKING
Markings for North America
Option A: (Zone System)
Ex ia IIC T4 (Canada)
Class I Zone 0 AEx ia IIC T4 (U.S.)
Flammable gas or vapour
Area classification
Conformity to U.S. requirements
Explosion protected
Protection method –
(intrinsic safety)
Gas group (acetylene &
hydrogen)
Temperature
Code
Class I   Zone 0   A   Ex   ia   IIC   T4
Option B: (Division System)
Flammable gas or vapour
Area classification
Gas group –
A: acetylene
B: hydrogen
C: ethylene
D: propane
Temperature
Code
Class I   Division 1   Groups A, B, C, D   T4

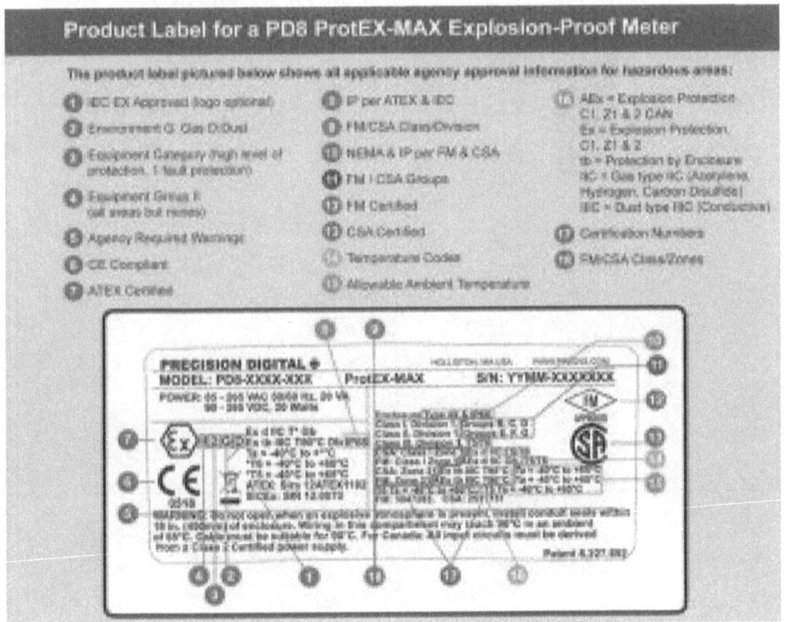

Product Label for a PD8 ProtEX-MAX Explosion-Proof Meter
This product label pictured below shows all applicable agency approval information for hazardous areas:
IEC EX Approval (logo optional)
Environment G: Gas D: Dust
Equipment Category (high level of protection, 1 fault protection)
Equipment Group II (all areas but mines)
Agency Required Warnings
CE Compliant
ATEX Certified
IP per ATEX & IEC
FM/CSA Class/Division
NEMA & IP per FM & CSA
FM / CSA Groups
FM Certified
CSA Certified
Temperature Codes
Allowable Ambient Temperature
AEx = Explosion Protection
Cl, Z1 & 2 CAN
Ex = Explosion Protection
Cl, Z1 & 2
tb = Protection by Enclosure
IIC = Gas type IIC (Acetylene,
Hydrogen, Carbon Disulfide)
IIIC = Dust type IIIC (Conductive)
Certification Numbers
FM/CSA Class/Zones
PRECISION DIGITAL
MODEL: PD8-XXXX-XXX   ProtEX-MAX   S/N: YYMM-XXXXXXX
Patent 5,327,001

	**ATEX II 2G EEx ia IIC T4** **Operating Temp. Range -20°** **to + 50°C** **IP30** *II= group II equipment* *2= Category 2* *G= Gas environment* *E=CENELEC Approved* *Ex= Explosion protected* *ia= Intrinsically safe for zone 0,1,2,* *IIC= Gas group-Hydrogen* *T4=Temperature class* *IP30= 3= Protected from solid* *=0 = No protection from liquid*
	**ATEX II 2 G EEx ia IIC T4** **-5ºC to +55ºC (+23ºF to** **+131ºF)** **IP20.** *II= group II equipment* *2= Category 2* *G= Gas environment* *E=CENELEC Approved* *Ex= Explosion protected* *ia= Intrinsically safe for zone 0,1,2,* *IIC= Gas group-Hydrogen* *T4=Temperature class* *IP20= 2= Protected from solid* *=0=No protection from liquid*

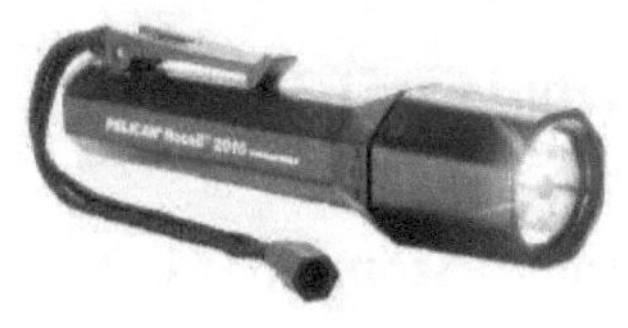	**TEX II 3 G EEx nL IIC T4 135°C** *II= group II equipment* *3= Category 3* *G= Gas environment* *E=CENELEC Approved* *Ex= Explosion protected* *nL= Special protection for zone 2,* *IIC= Gas group-Hydrogen* *$T_4$135=Temperature class* *IP30= 3= Protected from solid* *=0 = No protection from liquid*
	**ATEX II 2 G EEx ed IIC T4/T3** **ATEX II 2 D IP 65 T145 °C** *II= group II equipment* *2= Category 2* *G= Gas environment* *D= Dust environment* *E=CENELEC Approved* *Ex= Explosion protected* *ed=e= increased safety,=d flameproof for zone 1, 2.* *IIC= Gas group-Hydrogen* *T4/T3=Temperature class* *IP65= 6= Protected from solid* *=5=protection from liquid*

CHAPTER TWENTY

EQUIPMENT PROTECTION LEVELS – EPL

From 2007 onwards, the IEC Technical Standards in the series IEC 60079, and in particular IEC 60079 Part 14, have recognized that there may be occasions where it is necessary to increase, above the normal levels, the protection against ignition sources. This concept allows for consideration of risk (i.e. consequences of an explosion) as opposed to just the probability of a flammable atmosphere existing - the conventional selection criteria between the types of protection and the zone of use.

Three Equipment Protection Levels are specified as shown in the table below.

In normal circumstances the effect of these EPLs will be to retain the normal zone/equipment protection relationship. If, however, the risk is considered especially severe, then the required EPL for the zone may be increased. Similarly, if the risk is deemed to be especially small or negligible, the EPL may be reduced from the normal.

The following two tables show the normal relationship between EPL and zone, and the EPL awarded to each type of protection.

EQUIPMENT PROTECTION LEVEL

Equipment Protection Level (EPL)	Normal Applicable Zone(s)
Ga	0 (and 1 and 2)
Gb	1 (and 2)
Gc	2

20.1 EQUIPMENT AND PROTECTION LEVEL

Equipment Code	Description	EPL
Ex ia	Intrinsic safety 'ia'	Ga
Ex ib	Intrinsic safety 'ib'	Gb
Ex ic	Intrinsic Safety 'ic'	Gc
Ex d	Flameproof protection	Gb
Ex p	Purge/pressurized protection	Gb
Ex px	Purge/pressurized protection 'px'	Gb
Ex py	Purge/pressurized protection 'py'	Gb
Ex pz	Purge/pressurized protection 'pz'	Gc
Ex e	Increased safety	Gb
Ex m	Encapsulation	Gb
Ex ma	Encapsulation	Ga
Ex mb	Encapsulation	Gb
Ex o	Oil immersion	Gb
Ex q	Sand / powder (quartz) filling	Gb
Ex n	Type - n protection	Gc
Ex s	Special protection	Refer to equipment marking and documentation

CHAPTER TWENTY ONE

INGRESS PROTECTION (IP)

A sample of **IP68** means (as in the table below)

IP	6	8
"Ingress Protection"	First Digit: Solids Protection	Second Digit: Liquids Protection

The IP Code (or **International Protection Rating**, sometimes also interpreted as **Ingress Protection Rating***) consists of the letters IP followed by two digits and an optional letter. As defined in international standard IEC 60529, it classifies the degrees of protection provided against the intrusion of solid objects (including body parts like hands and fingers), dust, accidental contact, and water in electrical enclosures. The standard aims to provide users more detailed information than vague marketing terms such as waterproof.

The digits (characteristic numerals) indicate conformity with the conditions summarized in the tables below. For example, an electrical socket rated IP22 is protected against insertion of fingers and will not be damaged or become unsafe during a specified test in which it is exposed to vertically or nearly vertically dripping water.

IP22 or 2X are typical minimum requirements for the design of electrical accessories for indoor use.

FIRST DIGIT: SOLIDS (e.g. IP68, 6 is for solid)
The first digit indicates the level of protection that the enclosure provides against access to hazardous parts (e.g., electrical conductors, moving parts) and the ingress of solid foreign objects.

Level	Object size protected against	Effective against
0	Not protected	No protection against contact and ingress of objects
1	>50mm	Any large surface of the body, such as the back of the hand, but no protection against deliberate contact with a body part.
2	>12.5mm	Fingers or similar objects.
3	>2.5mm	Tools, thick wires, etc.
4	>1mm	Most wires, screws, etc.
5	Dust Protected	Ingress of dust is not entirely prevented, but it must not enter in sufficient quantity to interfere with the satisfactory operation of the equipment; complete protection against contact.

| 6 | Dust Tight | No ingress of dust; complete protection against contact. |

SECOND DIGIT: LIQUIDS (e.g. IP68, 8 is for liquid)

Protection of the equipment inside the enclosure against harmful ingress of water.

Level	Object size protected against	Effective against
0	Not protected	–
1	Dripping water	Dripping water (vertically falling drops) shall have no harmful effect.
2	Dripping water when tilted up to 15°	Vertically dripping water shall have no harmful effect when the enclosure is tilted at an angle up to 15° from its normal position.
3	Spraying water	Water falling as a spray at any angle up to 60° from the vertical shall have no harmful effect.
4	Splashing water	Water splashing against the enclosure from any direction shall have no harmful effect.
5	Water jets	Water projected by a nozzle (6.3mm) against enclosure from any direction shall have no harmful effects.

6	Powerful water jets	Water projected in powerful jets (12.5mm nozzle) against the enclosure from any direction shall have no harmful effects.
7	Immersion up to 1m	Ingress of water in harmful quantity shall not be possible when the enclosure is immersed in water under defined conditions of pressure and time (up to 1 m of submersion).
8	Immersion beyond 1m	The equipment is suitable for continuous immersion in water under conditions which shall be specified by the manufacturer. Normally, this will mean that the equipment is hermetically sealed. However, with certain types of equipment, it can mean that water can enter but only in such a manner that it produces no harmful effects.

21.1 IP RATING REFERENCE CHART

Below is an easy to follow reference chart to help you decide which IP rating you need or have.

IP Number	First Digit - SOLIDS	Second Digit - LIQUIDS

IP00	Not protected from solids.	Not protected from liquids.
IP01	Not protected from solids.	Protected from condensation.
IP02	Not protected from solids.	Protected from water spray less than 15 degrees from vertical.
IP03	Not protected from solids.	Protected from water spray less than 60 degrees from vertical.
IP04	Not protected from solids.	Protected from water spray from any direction.
IP05	Not protected from solids.	Protected from low pressure water jets from any direction.
IP06	Not protected from solids.	Protected from high pressure water jets from any direction.
IP07	Not protected from solids.	Protected from immersion between 15 centimeters and 1 meter in depth.
IP08	Not protected from solids.	Protected from long term immersion up to a specified pressure.
IP10	Protected from touch by hands greater than 50 millimeters.	Not protected from liquids.
IP11	Protected from touch by hands	Protected from condensation.

	greater than 50 millimeters.	
IP12	Protected from touch by hands greater than 50 millimeters.	Protected from water spray less than 15 degrees from vertical.
IP13	Protected from touch by hands greater than 50 millimeters.	Protected from water spray less than 60 degrees from vertical.
IP14	Protected from touch by hands greater than 50 millimeters.	Protected from water spray from any direction.
IP15	Protected from touch by hands greater than 50 millimeters.	Protected from low pressure water jets from any direction.
IP16	Protected from touch by hands greater than 50 millimeters.	Protected from high pressure water jets from any direction.
IP17	Protected from touch by hands greater than 50 millimeters.	Protected from immersion between 15 centimeters and 1 meter in depth.
IP18	Protected from touch by hands	Protected from long term immersion up to a specified pressure.

	greater than 50 millimeters.	
IP20	Protected from touch by fingers and objects greater than 12 millimeters.	Not protected from liquids.
IP21	Protected from touch by fingers and objects greater than 12 millimeters.	Protected from condensation.
IP22	Protected from touch by fingers and objects greater than 12 millimeters.	Protected from water spray less than 15 degrees from vertical.
IP23	Protected from touch by fingers and objects greater than 12 millimeters.	Protected from water spray less than 60 degrees from vertical.
IP24	Protected from touch by fingers and objects greater than 12 millimeters.	Protected from water spray from any direction.
IP25	Protected from touch by fingers	Protected from low pressure water jets from any direction.

	and objects greater than 12 millimeters.	
IP26	Protected from touch by fingers and objects greater than 12 millimeters.	Protected from high pressure water jets from any direction.
IP27	Protected from touch by fingers and objects greater than 12 millimeters.	Protected from immersion between 15 centimeters and 1 meter in depth.
IP28	Protected from touch by fingers and objects greater than 12 millimeters.	Protected from long term immersion up to a specified pressure.
IP30	Protected from tools and wires greater than 2.5 millimeters.	Not protected from liquids.
IP31	Protected from tools and wires greater than 2.5 millimeters.	Protected from condensation.
IP32	Protected from tools and wires	Protected from water spray less than 15 degrees from vertical.

	greater than 2.5 millimeters.	
IP33	Protected from tools and wires greater than 2.5 millimeters.	Protected from water spray less than 60 degrees from vertical.
IP34	Protected from tools and wires greater than 2.5 millimeters.	Protected from water spray from any direction.
IP35	Protected from tools and wires greater than 2.5 millimeters.	Protected from low pressure water jets from any direction.
IP36	Protected from tools and wires greater than 2.5 millimeters.	Protected from high pressure water jets from any direction.
IP37	Protected from tools and wires greater than 2.5 millimeters.	Protected from immersion between 15 centimeters and 1 meter in depth.
IP38	Protected from tools and wires greater than 2.5 millimeters.	Protected from long term immersion up to a specified pressure.
IP40	Protected from tools and small wires greater	Not protected from liquids.

	than 1 millimeter.	
IP41	Protected from tools and small wires greater than 1 millimeter.	Protected from condensation.
IP42	Protected from tools and small wires greater than 1 millimeter.	Protected from water spray less than 15 degrees from vertical.
IP43	Protected from tools and small wires greater than 1 millimeter.	Protected from water spray less than 60 degrees from vertical.
IP44	Protected from tools and small wires greater than 1 millimeter.	Protected from water spray from any direction.
IP45	Protected from tools and small wires greater than 1 millimeter.	Protected from low pressure water jets from any direction.
IP46	Protected from tools and small	Protected from high pressure water jets from any direction.

	wires greater than 1 millimetre.	
IP47	Protected from tools and small wires greater than 1 millimetre.	Protected from immersion between 15 centimetres and 1 meter in depth.
IP48	Protected from tools and small wires greater than 1 millimetre.	Protected from long term immersion up to a specified pressure.
IP50	Protected from limited dust ingress.	Not protected from liquids.
IP51	Protected from limited dust ingress.	Protected from condensation.
IP52	Protected from limited dust ingress.	Protected from water spray less than 15 degrees from vertical.
IP53	Protected from limited dust ingress.	Protected from water spray less than 60 degrees from vertical.
IP54	Protected from limited dust ingress.	Protected from water spray from any direction.

IP55	Protected from limited dust ingress.	Protected from low pressure water jets from any direction.
IP56	Protected from limited dust ingress.	Protected from high pressure water jets from any direction.
IP57	Protected from limited dust ingress.	Protected from immersion between 15 centimetres and 1 meter in depth.
IP58	Protected from limited dust ingress.	Protected from long term immersion up to a specified pressure.
IP60	Protected from total dust ingress.	Not protected from liquids.
IP61	Protected from total dust ingress.	Protected from condensation.
IP62	Protected from total dust ingress.	Protected from water spray less than 15 degrees from vertical.
IP63	Protected from total dust ingress.	Protected from water spray less than 60 degrees from vertical.
IP64	Protected from total dust ingress.	Protected from water spray from any direction.

IP65	Protected from total dust ingress.	Protected from low pressure water jets from any direction.
IP66	Protected from total dust ingress.	Protected from high pressure water jets from any direction.
IP67	Protected from total dust ingress.	Protected from immersion between 15 centimetres and 1 meter in depth.
IP68	Protected from total dust ingress.	Protected from long term immersion up to a specified pressure.
IP69K	Protected from total dust ingress.	Protected from steam-jet cleaning.

IP Number	First Digit - SOLIDS	Second Digit - LIQUIDS
IP00	Not protected from solids.	Not protected from liquids.
IP01	Not protected from solids.	Protected from condensation.
IP02	Not protected from solids.	Protected from water spray less than 15 degrees from vertical.
IP03	Not protected from solids.	Protected from water spray less than 60 degrees from vertical.

IP04	Not protected from solids.	Protected from water spray from any direction.
IP05	Not protected from solids.	Protected from low pressure water jets from any direction.
IP06	Not protected from solids.	Protected from high pressure water jets from any direction.
IP07	Not protected from solids.	Protected from immersion between 15 centimetres and 1 meter in depth.
IP08	Not protected from solids.	Protected from long term immersion up to a specified pressure.
IP10	Protected from touch by hands greater than 50 millimetres.	Not protected from liquids.
IP11	Protected from touch by hands greater than 50 millimetres.	Protected from condensation.
IP12	Protected from touch by hands greater than 50 millimetres.	Protected from water spray less than 15 degrees from vertical.

IP13	Protected from touch by hands greater than 50 millimetres.	Protected from water spray less than 60 degrees from vertical.
IP14	Protected from touch by hands greater than 50 millimetres.	Protected from water spray from any direction.
IP15	Protected from touch by hands greater than 50 millimetres.	Protected from low pressure water jets from any direction.
IP16	Protected from touch by hands greater than 50 millimetres.	Protected from high pressure water jets from any direction.
IP17	Protected from touch by hands greater than 50 millimetres.	Protected from immersion between 15 centimetres and 1 meter in depth.
IP18	Protected from touch by hands greater than 50 millimetres.	Protected from long term immersion up to a specified pressure.
IP20	Protected from touch by fingers and objects greater than 12 millimetres.	Not protected from liquids.

IP21	Protected from touch by fingers and objects greater than 12 millimetres.	Protected from condensation.
IP22	Protected from touch by fingers and objects greater than 12 millimetres.	Protected from water spray less than 15 degrees from vertical.
IP23	Protected from touch by fingers and objects greater than 12 millimetres.	Protected from water spray less than 60 degrees from vertical.
IP24	Protected from touch by fingers and objects greater than 12 millimetres.	Protected from water spray from any direction.
IP25	Protected from touch by fingers and objects greater than 12 millimetres.	Protected from low pressure water jets from any direction.
IP26	Protected from touch by fingers and objects greater than 12 millimetres.	Protected from high pressure water jets from any direction.
IP27	Protected from touch by fingers and objects greater than 12 millimetres.	Protected from immersion between 15 centimetres and 1 meter in depth.

IP28	Protected from touch by fingers and objects greater than 12 millimetres.	Protected from long term immersion up to a specified pressure.
IP30	Protected from tools and wires greater than 2.5 millimetres.	Not protected from liquids.
IP31	Protected from tools and wires greater than 2.5 millimetres.	Protected from condensation.
IP32	Protected from tools and wires greater than 2.5 millimetres.	Protected from water spray less than 15 degrees from vertical.
IP33	Protected from tools and wires greater than 2.5 millimetres.	Protected from water spray less than 60 degrees from vertical.
IP34	Protected from tools and wires greater than 2.5 millimetres.	Protected from water spray from any direction.
IP35	Protected from tools and wires greater than 2.5 millimetres.	Protected from low pressure water jets from any direction.

IP36	Protected from tools and wires greater than 2.5 millimetres.	Protected from high pressure water jets from any direction.
IP37	Protected from tools and wires greater than 2.5 millimetres.	Protected from immersion between 15 centimetres and 1 meter in depth.
IP38	Protected from tools and wires greater than 2.5 millimetres.	Protected from long term immersion up to a specified pressure.
IP40	Protected from tools and small wires greater than 1 millimetre.	Not protected from liquids.
IP41	Protected from tools and small wires greater than 1 millimetre.	Protected from condensation.
IP42	Protected from tools and small wires greater than 1 millimetre.	Protected from water spray less than 15 degrees from vertical.
IP43	Protected from tools and small wires greater than 1 millimetre.	Protected from water spray less than 60 degrees from vertical.

IP44	Protected from tools and small wires greater than 1 millimetre.	Protected from water spray from any direction.
IP45	Protected from tools and small wires greater than 1 millimetre.	Protected from low pressure water jets from any direction.
IP46	Protected from tools and small wires greater than 1 millimetre.	Protected from high pressure water jets from any direction.
IP47	Protected from tools and small wires greater than 1 millimetre.	Protected from immersion between 15 centimetres and 1 meter in depth.
IP48	Protected from tools and small wires greater than 1 millimetre.	Protected from long term immersion up to a specified pressure.
IP50	Protected from limited dust ingress.	Not protected from liquids.
IP51	Protected from limited dust ingress.	Protected from condensation.
IP52	Protected from limited dust ingress.	Protected from water spray less than 15 degrees from vertical.

IP53	Protected from limited dust ingress.	Protected from water spray less than 60 degrees from vertical.
IP54	Protected from limited dust ingress.	Protected from water spray from any direction.
IP55	Protected from limited dust ingress.	Protected from low pressure water jets from any direction.
IP56	Protected from limited dust ingress.	Protected from high pressure water jets from any direction.
IP57	Protected from limited dust ingress.	Protected from immersion between 15 centimetres and 1 meter in depth.
IP58	Protected from limited dust ingress.	Protected from long term immersion up to a specified pressure.
IP60	Protected from total dust ingress.	Not protected from liquids.
IP61	Protected from total dust ingress.	Protected from condensation.
IP62	Protected from total dust ingress.	Protected from water spray less than 15 degrees from vertical.
IP63	Protected from total dust ingress.	Protected from water spray less than 60 degrees from vertical.

IP64	Protected from total dust ingress.	Protected from water spray from any direction.
IP65	Protected from total dust ingress.	Protected from low pressure water jets from any direction.
IP66	Protected from total dust ingress.	Protected from high pressure water jets from any direction.
IP67	Protected from total dust ingress.	Protected from immersion between 15 centimetres and 1 meter in depth.
IP68	Protected from total dust ingress.	Protected from long term immersion up to a specified pressure.
IP69K	Protected from total dust ingress.	Protected from steam-jet cleaning.

CHAPTER TWENTY TWO

CHEMISTRY OF FIRE/EXPLOSION

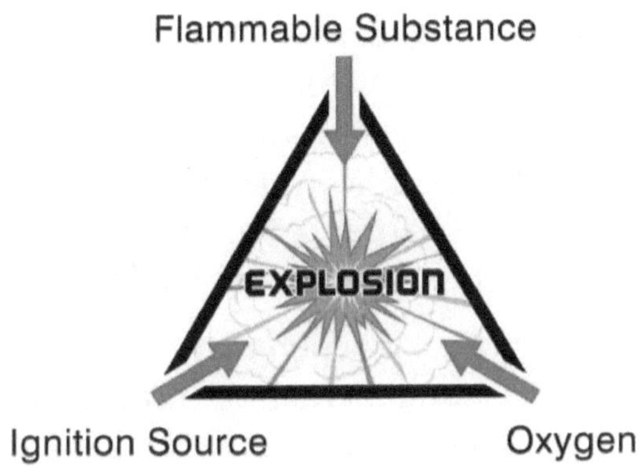

The **Fire Triangle** or **Combustion Triangle** is a simple model for understanding the necessary ingredients for most fires.

Fire is the rapid oxidation of a material in the exothermic chemical process of combustion, releasing heat, light, and various reaction product. Slower oxidative processes like rusting or digestion are not included by this definition.

The triangle illustrates the three elements a fire needs to ignite: heat, fuel and an oxidizing agent. A fire naturally occurs when the elements are present and combined in the right mixture meaning that fire is actually an event rather than a thing. A fire can be prevented or extinguished by removing any one of the elements in the fire triangle. For example, covering a fire with a fire blanket removes the oxygen part of the triangle and can extinguish a fire.

The fire tetrahedron represents the addition of a component in the chemical chain reaction, to the three already present in the fire triangle. Once a fire has started, the resulting exothermic chain reaction sustains the fire and allows it to continue until or unless at least one of the elements of the fire is blocked. Foam can be used to deny the fire the oxygen it needs. Water can be used to lower the temperature of the fuel below the ignition point or to remove or disperse the fuel. Halon can be used to remove free radicals and create a barrier of inert gas in a direct attack on the chemical reaction responsible for the fire.

Combustion is the chemical reaction that feeds a fire more heat and allows it to continue. When the fire involves burning metals like lithium, magnesium, titanium etc. (known as a class- D fire), it becomes even more important to consider the energy release. The metals react faster with water than with oxygen and thereby more energy is released. Putting water on such a fire results in the fire getting hotter or even exploding. Carbon dioxide extinguishers are ineffective against certain metals such as titanium. Therefore, inert agents (e.g. dry sand) must be used to break the chain reaction of metallic combustion.

In the same way, as soon as one of the four elements of the tetrahedron is removed, combustion stops.

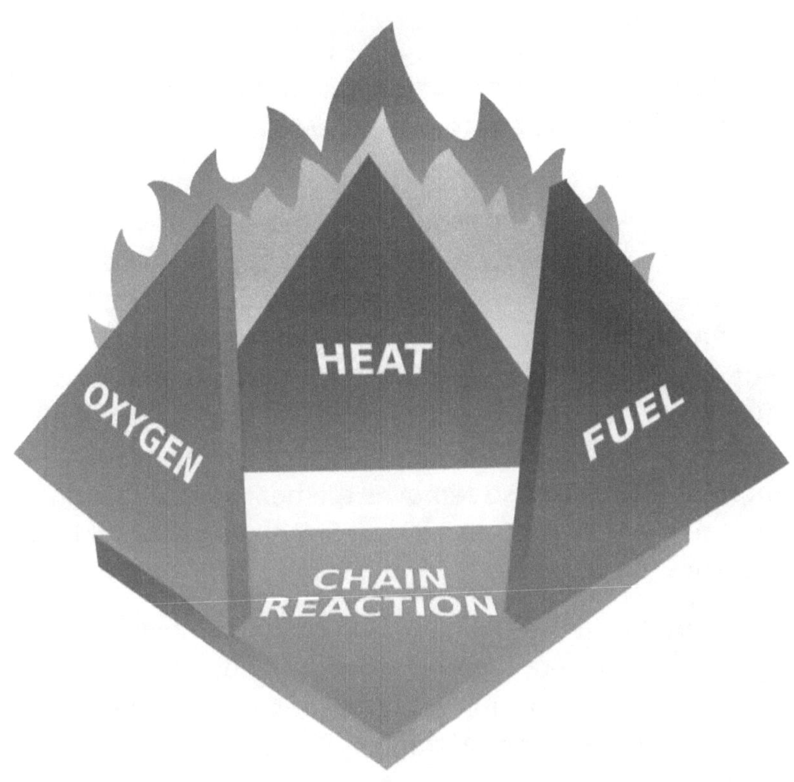

OXIDIZERS:

The oxidizer is the other reactant of the chemical reaction. In most cases, it is the ambient air, and in particular one of its components, oxygen (O_2). By depriving a fire of air, it can be extinguished; for example, when covering the flame of a small candle with an empty glass, fire stops; to the contrary, if air is blown over a wood fire with bellows, the fire is activated by the introduction of more air.

A fire based on a reaction with these oxidisers can be very difficult to put out until the oxidiser is exhausted; that leg of the fire triangle cannot be broken by normal means (i.e., depriving it of air will not smother it).

To stop a combustion reaction, one of the three elements of the fire-triangle has to be removed.

Without sufficient heat, a fire cannot begin, and it cannot continue. Heat can be removed by the application of a substance which reduces the amount of heat available to the fire reaction. This is often water, which absorbs heat for phase change from water to steam. Introducing sufficient quantities and types of powder or gas in the flame reduces the amount of heat available for the fire reaction in the same manner. Scraping embers from a burning structure also removes the heat source. Turning off the electricity in an electrical fire removes the ignition source.

Without fuel, a fire will stop. Fuel can be removed naturally, as where the fire has consumed all the burnable fuel, or manually, by mechanically or chemically removing the fuel from the fire. Without sufficient oxygen, a fire cannot begin, and it cannot continue.

CHAPTER TWENTY THREE

IGNITION SOURCES

An **ignition source** is a process or event which can cause a fire or explosion. An explosion can occur when flammable gases or vapours in the air come in contact with an **ignition source** such as a spark

Ignition sources include:

- Flames; Direct fired space and process heating; Use of cigarettes/matches, Cutting and welding flames, Hot surfaces, Heated process vessels such as dryers and furnaces, Hot process vessels, Space heating equipment, Mechanical machinery, Electrical equipment and lights, Mobile Phones and cameras.

Others include: Spontaneous heating, Friction heating or sparks, Impact sparks, Sparks from electrical equipment, Stray currents from electrical equipment & Electrostatic discharge sparks, Lightning strikes, Electromagnetic radiation of different wavelengths, and vehicles

23.1 IGNITION CONTROL

Sources of ignition should be effectively controlled in all hazardous areas by a combination of design measures, and systems of work:

- Using electrical equipment and instrumentation classified for the zone in which it is located. New mechanical equipment will need to be selected in the same way;

- Earthen of all plant/ equipment.

- Elimination of surfaces below auto-ignition temperatures of flammable materials being handled/stored.

- Provision of lightning protection;

- Correct selection of vehicles/internal combustion engines that have to work in the zoned areas.

- Correct selection of equipment to avoid high intensity electromagnetic radiation sources, e.g. limitations on the power input to fiber optic systems, avoidance of high intensity lasers or sources of infrared radiation.

- Prohibition of smoking/use of matches/lighters.

- Controls over the use of normal vehicles.

- Controls over activities that create intermittent hazardous areas, e.g. tanker loading/unloading

- Control of maintenance activities that may cause sparks/hot surfaces/naked flames through a Permit to Work System.

- Precautions to control the risk from pyrophoric scale, usually associated with formation of ferrous sulphide inside process equipment.

- Nonuse of mobile handsets and camera not properly rated within the facility.

23.2 EXPLOSION PREVENTION

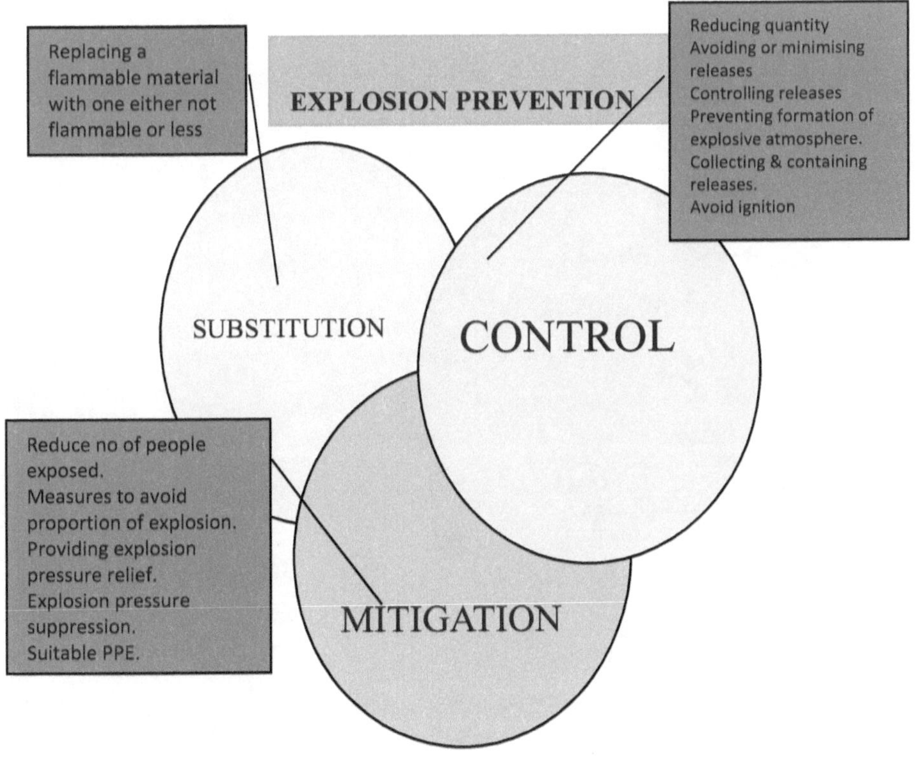

23.3 PREVENTION OF IGNITION

- Prevent contact between explosive mixture and ignition source.

- Limit energy of possible ignition source.

- Limit temperature of hot surfaces.

23.4 PROPAGATION OF EXPLOSION.

Limit propagation of Explosion through:

1. Flame Arrestors.
2. Gaps in Equipment housings
3. Extinguish & Suppress.
4. Bursting Discs.

CHAPTER TWENTY FOUR

1. **Iriama Pipeline Fire/Explosion Incident.**
    Occurred on Nov 13 2008 at around 1600hrs at
    a spill recovery & pipeline repairs site along the
    24" Amukpe-Sapele Trunk line, Sapele,
    Nigeria.

2. Rig: Bombay High North Platform
Date: 27 July 2005
Location: Bombay High, Indian Ocean
Operator: Oil and Natural Gas Corporation (ONGC)
Fatalities: 22

3. **PIPER ALPHA – NORTH SEA OFFSHORE PLATFORM.**
Fatalities: 167.

4. In India, The Bhopal gas tragedy occurred in December
   1984 wherein approximately 41 tonnes of deadly MIC
   was released in the dead of night.
   It caused the death of over 3000 people and continued
   life-long misery for over 300,000 with certain genetic
   defects passed on to the next generation

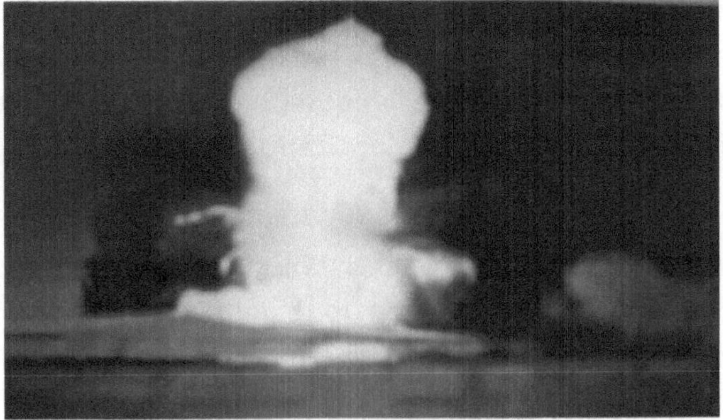

5. On June 1, 1974 a vapour cloud explosion destroyed
   the Nypro cyclohexane oxidation plant at Flixborough,
   England killing 28 people. Other plants on the site were
   seriously damaged or destroyed and the site presented
   a scene of utter devastation. The accident was traced
   to a poorly qualified design team that were asked to
   design and install temporary piping.

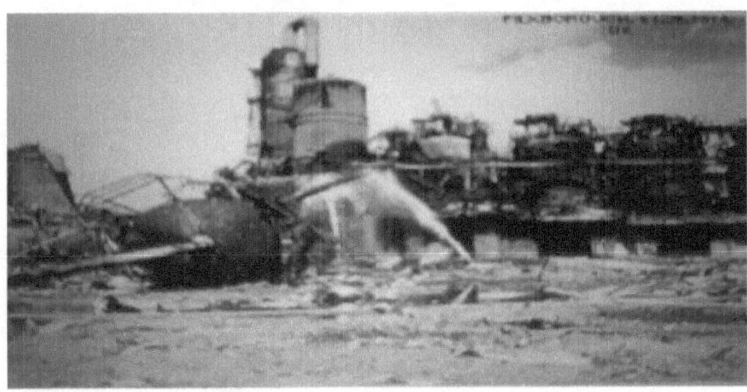

CHAPTER TWENTY FIVE

REGULATORY STANDARDS

There are various standards which give details of hazardous area requirements. In the main, the **International Electrotechnical Commission** (IEC) standards are now parallel voted by **Comité Européen de Normalisation Électrotechnique (European Committee for Electrotechnical Standardization)** (CENELEC).

It is important for equipment designers to design to the latest edition of **Atmosphères Explosibles** (ATEX) harmonized standards - the up to date list can be found on the EC(**Conformité Européenne (French for European Conformity)** ATEX website.

Gradually, the technical standards for the technology for gas/vapor hazards and those for dust hazards are being incorporated into the same series. For example IEC 60079-10 covers area classification IEC 60079-10-1 deals with gas/vapor hazards and IEC 60079-10-2 deals with dust hazards. Similar numbering will apply for other aspects such as installation